THE
POWER
OF
MERCURY

THE POWER OF MERCURY

Understanding Mercury Retrograde and Unlocking the Astrological Secrets of Communication

Leslie McGuirk

HARPERELIXIR

An Imprint of HarperCollinsPublishers

HARPER**ELIXIR**

HarperCollins books may be purchased for educational, business,
or sales promotional use. For information, please e-mail the
Special Markets Department at SPsales@harpercollins.com.

FIRST EDITION

Designed by Lucy Albanese
Zodiac icons, pages 34–39, 41–45, and 47: istock.com/PrettyVectors
Zodiac symbols appearing throughout: istock.com/Hollygraphic

Library of Congress Cataloging-in-Publication Data
Names: McGuirk, Leslie, author.
Title: The power of Mercury : understanding
  Mercury retrograde and unlocking the astrological
  secrets of communication / Leslie McGuirk.
Description: FIRST EDITION. | San
  Francisco : HarperElixir, 2016.
Identifiers: LCCN 2016028323 (print) | LCCN
  2016029329 (ebook) | ISBN 9780062434937
  (hardcover) | ISBN 9780062434951 (e-book)
Subjects: LCSH: Mercury (Planet)—Miscellanea. | Astrology.
Classification: LCC BF1724.2.M45 M34 2016 (print) |
  LCC BF1724.2.M45 (ebook) | DDC 133.5/33--dc23
LC record available at https://lccn.loc.gov/2016028323

19 20   LSC   10 9 8 7 6 5 4 3 2

To my mom, Marie McGuirk

CONTENTS

THE BLUEPRINT OF THE SOUL'S JOURNEY

WHEN I WAS NINETEEN, MY MOTHER SENT ME TO AN astrologer in Greenwich Village. This astrologer was, surprisingly, the daughter of an elegant older couple who lived in our WASP-y hometown of Bronxville, New York. Astrology was definitely not part of the culture of Bronxville. At that time in my life, I knew nothing about astrology. It seemed mystical and esoteric at best and at worst, made-up nonsense. I was skeptical about seeing this woman and assumed she was a fortune-teller; quite frankly, I was surprised that my mother wanted me to see her. But my mother knew this astrologer's parents, a refined older couple we used to see at church every Sunday. My mom had heard this astrologer give a talk at a women's luncheon in town.

She found her to be highly intelligent and persuasive—and it didn't hurt, in my mother's view, that she came from an upper-crust Bronxville family. Like many nineteen-year-olds, I was a little lost, and my mom figured a session with this astrologer might provide some direction.

When I arrived for my astrological reading, an attractive and wholesome-looking woman in her forties greeted me at the door of her small apartment. She sat me across from her at a small wooden table. On this table was a piece of paper with a big circle divided into twelve sections. Inside this circle were hand-drawn symbols that looked like hieroglyphics, along with lots of numbers with degree symbols next to them. The astrologer explained that this circle, or astrological wheel, was my natal chart—a map of the planets, the sun, and the moon at the date and time I was born, relative to the location of my birthplace. Everything was marked off with precise geometric measurements. She explained that this map of the heavens was a blueprint for my soul's journey. She said she would "read" my chart: interpret it to help me gain insight into my inner workings, which would help me make better choices for my life path. She also emphatically stated that I had free will. It was up to me to make my life a brilliant one. According to my natal chart, I would be well compensated (if I made correct choices) for some of the anguish I might have to experience in life. She told me I was a bit of a "stimulation junkie," where my brain was so overactive that I could easily turn down the wrong path and get involved with drugs or alcohol to quiet my overly stimulated mind. Or I could use my creative talents to become an artist and writer, and bring a lot of healing and joy to the world. Then she told me, "Most people are born with a wristwatch on their arm, but you were born carrying Big Ben. You will either use this intense power for tremendous good or you could implode and be very self-destructive."

She was right. I was intense. My family and friends could attest to that. My mother used to tell me all the time that I had more energy than my two sisters combined. My intensity always seemed to be a negative quality, but this astrologer made it seem as if it was a creative blessing. In my heart I always knew that I was creative, but a series of cruel grade-school teachers made me think otherwise. A pivotal moment occurred at age seven, when I drew a picture of a little boy at the beach and gave him a belly button. I started laughing because I thought it was funny. The teacher came to the back of the room and saw the belly button and proceeded to grab my arm and yank me to the front of the room, where she announced to the class that she didn't want to see any of us drawing belly buttons again. In that moment, my joy in creating art was snuffed out, and

I became hesitant to draw anything. As the years went on, I continued to doubt my creativity. In art classes, I made clouds purple and was told they had to be white, and was warned about putting red and green together because they clash. At home I would draw, but at school it never felt safe to creatively express myself.

Now here I was at age nineteen, sitting in a tiny New York City apartment with a total stranger, who seemed to know that I had squashed my creative energy and was terrified to express it. I had just transferred schools from an elite but very traditional liberal arts college to the decidedly unconventional Sarah Lawrence College, a shift about which I was very nervous. I had been proud to get into the elite school, but trauma after trauma followed me there. I was miserable and knew that I couldn't go back. It was my mom who suggested I try Sarah Lawrence, which was conveniently located in Bronxville—my hometown. The thought of living at home and going to Sarah Lawrence was not appealing at all. "Why would I want to go to that artsy-fartsy school?" I asked her, and added, "Weird people go there!" I didn't think of myself as the creative type at all. When I told the astrologer I had recently switched schools to Sarah Lawrence, she practically levitated with joy. Her exact words were "What a stroke of luck from the gods, because at Sarah Lawrence they will encourage your creativity."

Other than required art classes in grade school and high school, I had never taken any real classes in art or writing in my life. Here I was being told that not only was Sarah Lawrence a great fit, but I had to get busy immediately in the creative arts because I was destined to be an artist and writer. The astrologer said, "You don't have a minute to waste. You are getting a late start, but you can do it."

Hearing that was deeply powerful. The astrologer had such intense convictions and tremendous belief in my abilities. I wanted the type of life this astrologer envisioned for me. She described the possibilities on my horizon, including international travel, fame and fortune, meeting interesting creative people, and success in the publishing world. That singular reading came to inform all the choices that followed. I did go to Sarah Lawrence and found it to be incredibly inspiring. It was there that I learned how to think and express myself. Surrounded by wisdom keepers of the time, like Grace Paley and my fiction writing teacher, Allan Gurganus, I blossomed. For the first time in my life, I felt like there was something special inside of me that needed to be expressed. Because of the astrologer, I developed confidence in myself and my abilities and sought out the path of an artist and creator.

Heeding the astrologer's advice would be the single most important decision I made. She redirected my life in that one ninety-minute session. I believe she saved me from a lot of difficult times. I am not sure how long it would have taken me to find my way if I had not met her. I say this because now that I know how to read astrology charts, I can see what she saw when she met me at nineteen. My astrology chart shows a person with great abilities but also quite a few difficulties to overcome. Some people have a wide path to travel, and they can afford to make a few mistakes along the way. However, in my case, the path that would lead to my highest good was supernarrow. If I got off that path, it could be difficult. *For all of us, when we do what we are meant to do, our lives are easier. Astrology has the amazing capacity to indicate where the places of flow are indicated.*

After my reading, I wanted to learn everything about astrology. A stranger had been able to deliver so much accurate personal information, and I needed to know how she did it. More than coincidence was involved in her reading of my natal chart. She was able to make connections and bring clarity to my life that would have been difficult to uncover in any conventional way (this was the early '80s, after all, long before the dawn of the Google era). It was clear to me that there was some sort of machinery at work inside the astrological wheel.

The astrologer suggested I visit an occult bookstore in Manhattan called Weiser's. The word "occult" scared me—it made me think of witches and séances. It was the dead of winter when I stood outside Weiser's for the first time, wondering if it was safe to enter. Through the window, I saw a musty-looking store filled with shelves cramped with books. The guy behind the counter could have played the part of Merlin, with his long white hair and beard. Maybe he was a warlock who could read my mind and put a spell on me. As I walked in, I told myself that as long as I avoided the tarot cards and the more occult sections and headed straight to the astrology shelf, I would be safe. It seemed like there was science and math involved in astrology, which to my mind made it more accessible. At the same time, I couldn't help but sense that the books which towered around me in stacks explained the deep esoteric mysteries of how life worked.

I left Weiser's pretty quickly that day, with a few astrology books tucked in my bag, hoping one day I would be brave enough to spend more time there. There was still quite a bit of fear inside my heart around admitting, even to myself, that I was fascinated by the occult. I didn't know then that "occult" simply means that which is hidden or secret. Now I see that a fascination with the occult originates in the desire to better understand the mysteries of our human experience, for which astrology is such a powerful tool. It's been over thirty years since my first trip to

Weiser's, and in that time I've read several hundred books on astrology and metaphysics in general. One of the most rewarding aspects of studying astrology is that just when you think you've got a handle on something, you uncover another layer of knowledge. There are not enough days to learn it all, which is part of the pleasure—astrology challenges you to be a lifelong learner and to continue to grow and expand your worldview.

In my thirties I took my first official astrology class. Back then we didn't have the ability to easily do charts on the computer. The brilliant and patient teacher taught us how to calculate and draw charts by hand. We had to do all of the mathematical equations regarding the positions of the planets ourselves. It was a long and tedious process to set up a single chart. But learning how to construct a chart in this way helped me understand how much of astrology was like sacred geometry. It was nothing like tarot cards, and the more I studied the more I realized astrology was based on precise scientific measurements of where planets were in space relative to other planets. This was not like shuffling a deck of cards and interpreting pictures.

Meanwhile, my career as an artist and writer had taken off. Everything the astrologer said was true. I was writing children's books, and I had started my own company, McGuirk's Quirks, which produced an environmentally themed T-shirt line. *Glamour* magazine did a story on me and my company, and someone from Takashimaya, a high-end Japanese department store, saw this article. Soon I had a licensing agreement with Takashimaya whereby over 1,500 products were made with my designs. I was also chosen to be the designer for redecorating the official Tokyo Disneyland hotel. All the carpeting, wallpaper, bedspreads, and so on were based on my designs. The astrologer had said I would have success overseas, and she was right.

All along I continued to study astrology privately. By the time I was forty and living in Florida, I felt pretty confident about my astrological knowledge, but it wasn't something I felt comfortable sharing with many people. People knew me as an author of children's picture books and the owner of McGuirk's Quirks. In fact, only a handful of friends knew that I had studied astrology for most of my adult life. One night while I was hanging out at a local restaurant with some pals, the subject of astrology came up. One of my friends mentioned to the group that I could read charts. It turned out that one of the women there, whom I had never met before, was so horrified by my interest in astrology that she later told one of my friends that "Leslie is going to have nothing but bad things happening to her because she is doing the work of the devil." I was surely "going to go to hell."

Then there was the woman I hired to help organize my office who quit working for me when she saw that I had a lot of astrology books. This sixty-year-old person announced that because I did yoga and studied astrology, I was too close to the devil. When a local Florida magazine interviewed me about my career as a children's book author and illustrator, I told the writer how an astrologer had given me the push I needed to have a creative career. Then I realized I probably should not have told her this. "Please don't put that part about astrology in the magazine," I requested. I knew from personal experience that many people, especially in the South's Bible Belt, would have negative associations with astrology. I knew astrology wasn't witchcraft, but certainly where I lived in Florida, many people thought otherwise.

I used astrology for my own peace of mind and as a tool to better understand the people in my life. Once in a while, I would read a friend's chart if they were having a difficult time, because I found that astrology always offered a new way of looking at a situation. There was one friend in particular who found my reading of her chart very useful. She asked if I would teach an astrology class to a group of her friends. My first reaction was "Sure! That would be fun, but just don't tell too many people and please do not advertise it." She knew I was worried about being "found out," and I explained to her that being a children's book author and illustrator didn't exactly match up with being an astrologer. That first class of ten women was a big success. Most of them requested a private reading. Then these women started to tell their friends. Soon I was getting calls from friends of friends of friends. I remember exactly where I was in my living room when I realized the astrological readings were quickly filling up my calendar. I literally said a prayer to God: "If you want me to help people, I will. You can bring them to me. But I will not have a business card, or a website. I do not want to be an astrologer, but if I can help people, then let me be of service." I have never veered from this position. I have never actively looked for astrology clients. I am extremely clear that I am here to encourage and to guide. I take it as a huge honor to look at someone's chart. I feel a deep responsibility to always be positive, even when faced with people who have not had an easy time in life. With astrology, there is always a clear path, and the trick is getting our lives in sync with our soul's purpose.

Eventually my life path led me to teaching at Rancho La Puerta in Mexico, which has been rated by many travel magazines as one of the top destination spas in the world. At Rancho La Puerta I met the person who would be instrumental in getting me to write this very book—my future literary agent. She was definitely not a person who considered herself interested in astrology. But after attending one of my astrology lectures at the spa, she realized that the way I explained astrology actually made some sense. This wasn't the first time a "skeptic" told me I had opened their mind to the possibility that astrology was in fact very accurate as a diagnostic tool.

I think I've been able to connect with my clients and students because my approach to astrology is very different from what most people have experienced or what they expect astrology to be like, if they've been even slightly exposed to it. Astrology is a complex subject full of abstract ideas—and it doesn't help that a lot of its language sounds like jargon. It takes years to learn the language of astrology, and it can feel unnecessarily confusing and mysterious to nonexperts, which is pretty much everyone. But it doesn't have to be that way, and I don't believe it *needs* to be that way. Because of my background as a children's book author and illustrator, my brain has been trained to make complex ideas as simple and entertaining as possible. I tend not to use traditional astrological language to explain a client's chart. All that matters to me is sharing the incredible wisdom found in everyone's birth chart and helping them understand how to work with the gentle guiding forces of the cosmos for their highest good.

1

ASTROLOGY, THE LANGUAGE OF COMPASSION

WHEN USED CORRECTLY, ASTROLOGY IS THE LANGUAGE of compassion. It reveals how individuals are wired and how best to operate given that wiring. Understanding your wiring—and experiencing all that astrology can do for you—begins with having your natal chart read. The natal chart is the foundation of astrology. It is a diagram or map that plots out the placement of the sun, moon, and planets in the twelve signs of the zodiac at the moment you were born, based on where on the earth you took your first breath. Each planet, as well as the sun and the moon, correlates with a different aspect of your psychology, and the placement of the planet in the zodiac indicates how that psychological trait will be expressed. For example, we all have the planet Mars somewhere in our chart. Mars is the planet that rules our desires, our energy, and how we take action. How we express those behaviors will be colored by the zodiac constellation in which Mars landed at the time of your birth. So if Mars was in Cancer when you were born, you will have a very soft masculine side. There is nothing macho about Mars in Cancer. Each planet, as well as the sun and moon, and its placement in the zodiac has essential information to tell us about different aspects of ourselves. The whole chart is a magical dance of different energies. Sun sign astrology alone can't possibly get to the true essence of a person's being.

The astrological wheel that composes the natal chart has twelve sections. In astrological language these sections are called houses. But I think it is easier to think of them as twelve *rooms* inside a house. Each room is dedicated to a different part of your life, from family to work to money, etc. Imagine that on the door of the room is a sign that reads "Susan's Love Life" or "Susan's Career."

The planets and the sun and moon each live in a different room of the house. Think of it this way: the planets are like people. The zodiac signs are the clothes they wear. And where each person lives is decided by where they fall inside the astrology wheel—which distinct room of the house. The interpretation of these complex interactions makes up an astrology reading. An astrology chart reveals the basic psychological and behavioral patterns of an individual— the inherent qualities that drive but do not determine our decision making, which is also shaped by familial, cultural, and environmental influences, of course. Daily and monthly sun sign horoscopes could never be truly accurate because each individual natal chart is not only complex but also unique. To say that all Cancers should avoid travel in July, or that all Geminis might meet the love of their life during the month of August couldn't possibly have much validity. There can be a slight flavor of accuracy around the tone of what is occurring for all Cancers, or Leos, but in my opinion, magazine horoscopes are more for entertainment than anything else.

The astrology familiar in the West began around 2000 BC, when human beings watched the skies, using what they saw above as a tool to guide them through life. Following the stars was the method early sea-goers used to navigate the oceans. Early civilizations realized that planting seeds during certain moon phases made for better crops. The ancient Greek physician Hippocrates, regarded as the father of medicine, insisted that his students study astrology. He believed, in his words, "He who does not understand astrology is not a doctor but a fool." Carl Jung, the father of Jungian psychology, drew up astrology charts for all his patients.

Freud told him to avoid astrology because people would think he was crazy, but Jung replied that he couldn't do that because astrology was too accurate to ignore. Many great thinkers used elements of astrology in their work, including Paracelsus, Leonardo da Vinci, and Sir Isaac Newton.

From the very beginning, astrology combined science with spirituality. Astrologers were priests who studied the heavens looking for divine guidance. They took note of celestial patterns and understood there was a correlation between their bodies and what was going on above their heads. The biblical Three Wise Men, who brought gifts to the infant Jesus, were known as "Magi." The word "Magi" comes to us from Old Persia and describes the priestly caste of skilled astrologers. As the Magi began their journey to meet the newborn Jesus, they followed the star of Bethlehem, which was actually not a star but a rare planetary conjunction.

Despite this long history of humankind's relationship to the sky above, people have dismissed astrology as hocus pocus: a kind of fortune-telling likely to be performed by a woman looking into a crystal ball. This couldn't be more incorrect. Astrology does not tell us what will happen; it is not deterministic. It can't be, because we have free will. One can look at the patterns astrology reveals and make educated, and surprisingly accurate, predictions about what *might* happen in a person's life, but at the end of the day our decisions determine outcomes.

We would never accuse an auto mechanic of fortune-telling if they predicted a breakdown after looking at a car's owner's manual and seeing that it needed diesel fuel and the owner was about to put in gasoline. What if an astrology chart was the same as your car's owner's manual? Think of how useful it would be to know how best to operate your life so that everything ran more smoothly. Many people misunderstand the power of astrology. They think the planets rule our lives. This is especially true of the current fad of blaming Mercury retrograde for every failure or screw up. The truth is that astrology, especially Mercury retrograde, does not control our lives. The planets simply reflect aspects of what it means to be human. We are responsible for how we tune into the celestial energies. It is our choice to respond to the heavenly patterns with awareness. If it rains, you can scream and yell at the weather and blame the rain for your lousy day, but you made it lousy, not the rain. The rain was an influence but not the cause.

The cosmic currents do shape our experiences, just as weather does. The trick is to work with what is and not fight it. One of the best things about astrology is that it works: it helps us to read the "weather." We may never totally understand why it works, but we can still appreciate its beauty and its power. There is a flow to life. We have sunrises and sunsets, low tides and high tides—all of which are connected to the sun and moon. The planets have their own rhythm and flow, and our human part in this earthly system is connected to the solar system. Astrology is a way to map human design within this magical universal system.

Some of my students have asked me, "What about twins? Don't they have the exact same chart? How can they be different?" Imagine two red Mercedes convertibles coming off the assembly line. Like two identical twins, they are made at the same time, at the same place, with the same wiring systems. However, the minute you put a human being behind the wheel, all bets are off as to how these two cars will end up after ten years. One person could wait too long between oil changes or drive the Mercedes into a bad part of town, leave it there, and return to find it vandalized. Another person might keep their Mercedes garaged and be meticulous about all the maintenance. After ten years, if you put these two cars next to each other, how different would they be? Same car, but with different owners there would be different outcomes. What happens in your life is up to you. No one can tell you what to do. You have to live your own life.

A professional astrologer is like an orchestra conductor who holds a baton and moves his arm but has no real control over the instruments in the orchestra pit. He is not the one making the music. His job is to make everything flow as smoothly as possible. The musicians have all the control, just as an individual has complete free will over all of his "instruments"—the implication of the placement of planets in our natal chart. We hold each planetary placement (each "instrument") with our own intentions, and how we use what we were given is up to us. We each possess a distinct "piece of music" (i.e., the intended course of our life), but how we play this music is up to us.

An astrologer can only tell you the best way to take what you've got and make what you want. An astrologer cannot and should not predict the future. All we can say is that the guitar needs restringing or the drums are overpowering the clarinet. Or we can say, "That tuba is so loud that if you don't tone it down, you are going to annoy everyone around you!" There is nothing inherently negative about that tuba. It is what we do with the tuba that makes all the difference. Some of us were born with very complicated musical scores. It can take twenty years to learn how to "play" just one part of your chart. Astrology can't impel, compel, or dispel. All an astrologer can do is see the patterns, hear the chords, listen for the resonances, and help the client respond with intention.

But like anything that has power, if put in the wrong

hands, astrology can do harm. Just as a knife can be a useful tool for cutting a loaf of bread, it can also be a weapon. How the knife is used is all about the intention of the person holding it. So there is every reason to be careful with astrology. Just as you would be judicious about what surgeon you allow to operate on you, you should use care when allowing someone to delve into your chart and thus your soul. In the wrong hands, your chart could be misread, and harmful things could be said. I have had clients repeat back to me incredibly hurtful "predictions" previous astrologers had forecast for them. One young woman in her forties told me that the only other astrologer she had seen (when she was twenty) had declared that she would never marry, because her seventh astrological house (of marriage) was empty. This woman was not married; she felt like the astrologer had put this thought in her head and thus it became true. This is plain cruelty and utterly wrong. When an area of the chart is empty, I believe it means that part of your life takes care of itself. Things should fall into place pretty easily in that sphere of your life. If someone tells you otherwise, and you believe him or her, however, then it may well "come true." Once something negative about your future is placed inside your head, you may make choices to realize that negative outcome. Humans are very complicated creatures and highly susceptible to language. What others tell us and what we tell ourselves can become the reality we live.

One of the greatest teachings astrology has given me is that there is nothing inherently negative in any chart, even when we see what looks to be a challenging aspect. One's attitude toward what one is dealt makes all the difference. You can either work with your wiring system or fight it your entire life. Often the people with gnarly charts have the most interesting life paths and do the most good on the planet. Those harsher aspects indicate where we have resistance, and it is those spots where we build muscle and get strong. Even if there are difficulties in a chart, which are completely normal, there is always a way "out." We are here on planet Earth to learn lessons. An astrology chart tells us what those lessons are.

I believe astrology is the language of compassion. Once you realize people are what they are, you do not try to change them. One can only hope that we each become the best we possibly can be. You would not get mad at a Jack Russell terrier for being yappy, or a Greyhound for being a fast runner; we are each wired to be a certain way. The goal is to learn the lessons indicated in the natal chart, and then outgrow the chart so that it has zero influence on us. I believe we are tested over and over again with similar lessons, until we catch on to what we are supposed to be learning. Once we learn that particular lesson, that series of tests is passed and we can move forward to the next level of lessons. The goal is to learn all the lessons indicated in the chart so that we can rise above the chart. The chart becomes like the skin the snake has shed. It used to be part of us, but it is no longer.

We don't have a choice regarding when we are born and what was directly above our heads. All we can do is realize we are all perfect exactly as we were made, and whatever challenges or gifts we were born with are part of a divine plan.

2

THE POWER OF MERCURY

WHEN YOU WERE BORN, MERCURY WAS CIRCLING around in the sky and passing through one of the twelve zodiac star formations, or constellations. We all know our sun sign. That is the zodiac constellation where the sun was positioned at the time of your birth. Your sun sign describes your basic personality traits. But it is too simplistic by a long shot to say that all Leos, for example, are alike. There are too many forces at work in the astrology chart for this to be true. In my opinion, if you want a specific understanding of a person's being, the first sign in your chart you should learn is your Mercury sign. Why? In astrology, the planet Mercury has dominion over everything related to how we communicate and how our minds process information.

Mercury informs how we use one of our most powerful human tools: words.

Your Mercury sign has much to teach you about how your mind works and how that shapes the way you relate and communicate to other people, both one-on-one and in groups. Are you sociable and a brilliant conversationalist? Do you grasp concepts easily? Are you able to jump ahead of people because your mind is working so fast? Do you need time to be introspective? Can you handle arguments well and stand your ground? Do you love to pitch ideas and sell concepts to others? Your Mercury sign can help you understand the answers to these questions—and why they matter. Very few of us know our Mercury sign, however.

In all my years studying astrology charts, I would say that knowing someone else's Mercury sign is of the utmost importance when it comes to happy partnerships of all types, because Mercury describes our intelligence, mind, and memory. It rules our sense of humor, what fascinates us, how we speak, how we write, and how we express ourselves in words. And in this day and age, it seems we are communicating all the time; whether we're talking or texting or emailing or posting to social media, we live in a hyperconnected world that relies on exchanging information, ideas, and words. Words are where we start.

Words are what make us different from other mammals. Our minds create thoughts, and we share our thoughts using words. This is all the territory of Mercury's influence, and I believe it is the one planet we should be checking on, even before the sun sign placement. You can determine a level of empathy by knowing a Mercury sign. You can figure out if someone is a careful, slow thinker or a zippy, quick-to-fire-off-a-comment kind of human. Mercury plays a crucial role in our lives because it colors our mental perceptions. It shows the way information is taken in, and how it is relayed back out. By looking at a Mercury placement you will know how a person would verbally comfort you, or conversely how they will argue. For all these reasons, Mercury's role in your life is at the very foundation of your entire being. What better way to know yourself and others than to understand how a person thinks? Mercury signs have a huge observable impact, especially when it comes to our relationship with others, because by knowing the Mercury signs you can tell what kind of back-and-forth energy two people will share.

Mercury is perhaps the most underweighted planet in the natal chart. Most astrologers give a lot of credence to the sun, moon, and rising (or ascendant) signs. But Mercury signs are rarely discussed, even though everyone talks about Mercury retrograde all the time. Mercury is the planet closest to the sun. It is also the smallest planet. It is quite speedy, taking just eighty-eight days to complete its rotation around the sun. From the earth, Mercury's path can look erratic, seeming to move both forward and backward. When it appears to be going backward, it really isn't. That is when Mercury is in retrograde. When we speak of someone as being mercurial, it means they move like the planet, in an ever-changing manner.

In Roman mythology, Mercury was messenger of the gods (in Greek mythology, he was known as Hermes). Mercury was the god of traders, merchants, and messengers, depicted with wings on his feet or on his helmet, symbolizing his swiftness. In his hand, he carried the caduceus, a staff with two snakes wrapped around it, symbolizing knowledge and wisdom, and representing the mind. The word "mercury" comes from the Latin root *merx*, which linguists describe as related to goods, trade, and wages—the realm of the merchant. Merchants and salespersons are often called "fast talking"—a description of their linguistic prowess and powers of persuasion. In addition to being a speedy messenger, Mercury was also a fantastic speaker and writer. Again, everything about the symbolism for Mercury relates to the power of words and our brains.

MERCURY, THE ELEMENTS, AND THE ZODIAC

Like the sun, the moon, and the other seven planets, Mercury has a specific placement in your natal chart, falling under one of the twelve zodiac signs. Each sign of the zodiac is associated with one of the four elements: fire, earth, air, or water. When you look up your Mercury sign (in the tables at the back of the book), you will notice that Mercury usually falls under the same zodiac sign as your sun sign, the zodiac sign before it, or the zodiac sign right after it. This is because in the sky, Mercury is always close to the sun. The zodiac sign under which your Mercury falls is your "Mercury sign." (When people say "I'm a Scorpio" or "I'm a Gemini" they are really telling you their *sun sign*—the placement of the sun in the zodiac on their natal chart— but every planet, along with the moon, has its own zodiac sign in your chart.) So if your Mercury is in Libra, you're a Mercury Libra. This means that the attributes and qualities of Libra will inform and shape how you communicate. And the element with which Libra is associated—air—will give you additional insight into how well you will communicate with another Mercury sign.

Before we get into the nitty-gritty of your Mercury sign, however, we need to begin with a fuller understanding of the zodiac signs and the elements. Remember your Mercury sign will fall into one of these twelve zodiac signs, so it is important to understand these basic archetypes. We all know our sun sign, which is in one of the twelve zodiac signs. Sun signs are like telling someone you are a Volvo or a Jaguar; it doesn't say if you are a station wagon or a convertible. A sun sign is just your "make," not your model, and your model is far more telling than your "make." Your model, and what is under the hood of your car, make up the ingredients of your vehicle. The other planets and their placements are where the guts of astrology truly lie.

When we look at Mercury, it is imperative that we remember it describes only one of the ways we connect with each other: through sounds and symbols known as words. How we use words and with what overall tone can vary greatly from person to person. We all have a way we make noise, which is what language basically is. We open our mouths and all these sounds come out. Think of the total miracle of language. Many believe that we all have a magical capacity to create our reality through words. Words are vibrations. There are many mind tools, like prayers, chants, and mantras associated with creating peace. We have a choice in how we use words, and there is always a skillful way and a not-so-skillful way. Words also have what the Tibetans call "wind energy." Imagine the wind energy of these words: cashmere, Galapagos, sarsaparilla. Now imagine these words: crotch, ketchup, pitchfork. The first are soft, flowing sounds. The second batch of words has an edge. Remember there is nothing right or wrong about any style of words. In this book we are dealing with an understanding of the various feeling tones that different Mercury combinations make. It is the placement of your Mercury in one of the twelve zodiac signs that shapes the kind of sounds you make—and how those sounds affect others. Once you identify your Mercury sign, you will understand that a zodiac sign colors your method of communicating. This is never going to change, just as a Mercedes will always be a Mercedes. There is nothing inherently negative about any Mercury placement. In this book, we will look at your individual Mercury placement combined with another person's Mercury placement to better understand your communication styles and thus your compatibility. Certain combinations are trickier than others. Some people are just naturally on the same wavelength.

Think of the twelve zodiac signs as being twelve different flavors of ice cream; some people are pistachio, some are coffee, some are peach, others are mint chocolate chip. Imagine that six of these flavors taste really great when paired up on a cone (not all at once!). But then when you mix them with one of the other six flavors, it leaves a less than pleasant taste in your mouth. Determining astrological compatibility is like that. All planets fall into one of the twelve zodiac signs. And each of these twelve signs falls into one of four elemental categories: FIRE, EARTH, AIR, and WATER. These elements refer to the vital forces, or energies, that make up our entire universe. Every planet falls into an elemental category. For the purposes of this book, you only need to know the element of your Mercury sign (which you can look up in the tables at the back of this book). Is the zodiac sign that your Mercury fell into a fire sign? earth? air? or water?

FIRE SIGNS	EARTH SIGNS	AIR SIGNS	WATER SIGNS
Aries	Taurus	Gemini	Cancer
Leo	Virgo	Libra	Scorpio
Sagittarius	Capricorn	Aquarius	Pisces

FIRE is all about energy. Fire signs are all about passion and basic instincts. People who have a Mercury fire sign express themselves with enthusiasm and warmth. They can also be very quick, and sometimes snarky, with their words, and just like fire they can burn and leave verbal singe marks on other people. Mercury fire placements can radiate faith and encouragement coupled with a strong drive to fix things or improve situations.

EARTH is all about being grounded. Earth signs are attuned with the world of physical form. People who have a Mercury earth sign have a practical, matter-of-fact way of dealing with the world. A Mercury placement in earth describes people who use language in a concrete and pragmatic fashion. There is a utilitarian aspect to this placement. Words are used to make specific points.

AIR is all about the mind. The element of air correlates with the world of thoughts and abstract ideas. People who have a Mercury air sign are usually talented communicators and writers. Since Mercury is all about communication, the planet is comfortable in air because there is a sympathetic resonance. Air can also be detached. Think of a bird in a tree. It has the bird's-eye view and a great overall perspective, but it can sometimes feel far away from those on the ground, so there is sometimes aloofness with air.

WATER is about emotions. Water signs symbolize the cooling, healing principles of water and are known for their heightened sensitivity and empathy. People who have a Mercury water sign are usually highly intuitive, and all thoughts are filtered through their feelings before logic. Words are usually used with gentle care in water sign Mercury placements. However, they can also hesitate to share their thoughts because of being so emotional. They dislike verbal conflicts, and will get into an argument only if forced to.

All you have to do is look to Mother Nature to figure out which elements are compatible. Fire and air signs are compatible. You can't have a fire without oxygen. Air and fire can't exist without the other. Earth and water signs are compatible. The plants can't survive without water, and the earth holds a lake. Furthermore, the oceans meet the beaches, so water meets earth naturally.

Water and earth are more self-contained than fire and air. Water and earth live more within themselves. They hold back on their energy and are more cautious. This way of being allows them to build a solid foundation for movement forward. Fire and air are far more expressive. They are always laying it out there, pouring forth their essential life force unabashedly—and sometimes ignoring limits completely. Fire and air are more direct and more social. Their verbal expression is more forthright.

If you mix fire with earth, or air with water, it is not necessarily a bad thing. It is just that there will be more intensity, and possibly more complications and less ease. In a romantic relationship, we are looking for what is easy and effortless (most of us, anyway!). By staying within your own elemental group, or one that is complementary, you are more likely to find a more comfortable and less stressful relationship. But please understand that even less than ideal combinations can be useful, as well as fun and filled with interesting life lessons.

For example, water puts out fire, and the heat of the sun (fire) evaporates water. There is a basic tension between these two elemental forces. However, fire and water can make steam, which can be nice! Or take air and water. Air can put bubbles into water, making it lighter, but a lot of air can whip up the water and make for rough seas. It all depends on the consciousness of the individuals involved. With awareness and compassion anything can work. The goal in this book is to figure out how to accept what is and work within the parameters of our basic natures.

Knowing the detailed traits of the twelve zodiac signs will help you better understand your Mercury placement. What follows is a short rundown on the basic traits of each zodiac sign.

ARIES: THE RAM

Being the first sign of the zodiac is an important clue to Aries traits: Aries wants to be first! Aggressive, determined, and driven like the ram, Aries wants what they want, when they want it. They have the energy of a young boy: impulsive, quick, and direct. Courageous to the point of daring, they possess a love of movement and adventure. Aries are excellent at starting projects but not always great at finishing them. If boredom sets in, they lose interest. They usually have sharp minds and enjoy a good debate. Since they are part of the fire team, Aries can easily lose their temper, blow up, but then get over it just as quickly. They do not hold grudges. Spirited and assertive, they may seem uncontrollable to others. They do not like being told they are wrong. But if you want some playful fun, Aries is with you all the way. They are always game for action, and you would never want to quell their enthusiastic natures. They are the ones who as children would say, "Look, Mom! No hands!"

LEO: THE LION

Leo is the "let me entertain you" sign of the zodiac. Think of the way lions behave. Even motionless, they still possess a powerful silent presence. Most Leos carry themselves in a regal way. Lions sleep about twenty-two hours every day, and yet they are muscular and have great physical strength. That explains a lot about Leo traits. They look and act impressive, yet barely have to do anything to get that way! They can also be kittenish and quite cuddly. They bring a sense of entitlement to everything they do. "Well of course I will be given the best table at the restaurant! Don't they know who I am?" Born to lead and light up a room, Leos are usually warm and magnanimous. Quite charismatic and pleasant to be around, they are good company as long as you are noticing them! They hate to be ignored. If you cross them, they will do what any cat does: their claws will come out and blood can flow. But if you want loyalty, elegance, and drama, Leos have that in abundance.

SAGITTARIUS: THE CENTAUR

The symbol for Sagittarius is the centaur, which is half horse and half man. This is a sign of contradictions, as the horse wants to be free and desires to travel great distances, and the man craves intellectual stimulation, which has nothing to do with the physicality of the lower part of the centaur's body. The centaur has a bow and arrow tipped with fire. They shoot, sometimes without thinking, and if not evolved, they couldn't care less where their arrows land. If evolved, Sagittarius is the great knowledge seeker. They quest for spiritual truths. They are the philosophers of the zodiac. Playful and fun loving, they bring their horsey sense of humor to all occasions. Freedom is of paramount importance to them. High spirited and somewhat temperamental, they are complicated creatures who appear impulsive one minute and then studious and bookwormish the next.

TAURUS: THE BULL

Taurus is the most down-to-earth, practical sign of the zodiac. This is a sign that values a comfortable, attractive, and safe environment, and would rather not experience any more change than is absolutely necessary. Like the symbol of their sign, Taureans can have a bullish disposition when provoked. You will think they are calm, passive, and contented, but if you disturb their peace and quiet they can get quite angry. It takes a lot to provoke them, but if you do, watch out! Like a solid hunk of granite, they can seem unmovable and resistant to change. They are rock-solid and dependable, you know you can count on them. They can also be very sentimental. Don't ever ask a Taurean to throw out something that has a special memory attached to it. They won't let go of anything until they are ready (and this includes people, objects, and memories). Do not push them to let go before they are comfortable, or they will get bullheaded. A fine appreciation of beauty and sensual pleasures is part of most Taureans' personalities. They often are creative and can exhibit an artistic flair even if it is just in how they set a table.

VIRGO: THE VIRGIN

Virgos are the sensitive, reserved sign of the zodiac—and they've been given an unfair bad rap. Their critical abilities are often seen as nitpicky. Their modest, cautious nature is often perceived as boring. The pleasure they receive from analyzing complex issues and distilling their essence has been called overly analytical. At the end of the day, where would any of us be without these Virgos who were born to be responsible? They are methodical by nature. And even though they often come across as calm and confident, they really are not. They probably have more self-doubt than any other sign. Their symbol is the female virgin, and she wants to "be good" and "do good" and is tough on herself if she isn't precise and dutiful. Virgo prefers to quietly observe. They keep their feelings to themselves, and because of this, others may find them cool and reserved. They really are kind and clear-thinking individuals who basically want to please. Yet their exacting and fastidious ways may feel perfectionist to others. However, these traits are very useful, as these are the people you want doing your taxes or reading the fine details of your legal document. Their conscientious ways are so strong that Virgos need to be careful of becoming fault-finding and too exacting on themselves and others. Getting a Virgo to stop working so hard and just play takes a bit of doing because their sense of duty is so strong.

CAPRICORN: THE GOAT

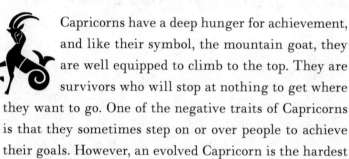

Capricorns have a deep hunger for achievement, and like their symbol, the mountain goat, they are well equipped to climb to the top. They are survivors who will stop at nothing to get where they want to go. One of the negative traits of Capricorns is that they sometimes step on or over people to achieve their goals. However, an evolved Capricorn is the hardest working, most persistent and courageous of all the signs. Their ruling planet is Saturn. Almost every word in the English language that begins with an "st" combination relates to Saturn and can be used to describe the traits of a Capricorn: structure, stability, strength, stamina, strong, steel, standards, and steadfast all relate to Capricorns. They are often born "old," and as they get older they become more youthful and lighter in spirit. These are the serious folks who are sometimes accused of having a too-saturnine personality. Yes, they are serious and earnest, but Capricorns will be equally intent on making sure they allow some frivolity in their lives. They come across as cautious and a bit reserved, but once you get to know them, they can be quite dynamic. Their initial reserve is not due to low self-esteem; they are just born with serious natures. They are trustworthy and dependable, and on the whole they have good, solid dispositions. Their biggest lesson is to allow for the impractical, the fanciful, and the whimsical. These are the realms that will help balance out their purposeful natures, because not everything in life has to be practical.

GEMINI: THE TWINS

 Geminis ooze charismatic charm. They have a wonderful way with words and are almost impossible to resist. Yet they may also use their keen intellect to confuse others as they flit in a million different directions, and they can be irritatingly hard to pin down. The problem with Geminis is that you never know which twin you are dealing with. Enthusiastic and abhorring routine, Geminis stay superbusy just to avoid boredom. Other signs might call them fickle, but it's just that Geminis love novelty. A new restaurant, a new gadget, or a new novel—whatever it might be, Geminis always show great interest in innovation. They are usually emotionally sensitive, but don't be surprised if one minute they are warm and affectionate and the next minute cool and indifferent. They will keep you guessing, that's for sure.

LIBRA: THE SCALES

Libra is the sign of partnership. Its symbol is the balanced scales of justice, so fairness is what they always strive for. This is the most composed, rational, and diplomatic sign of the zodiac, and sometimes Libras possess these traits to a fault. The only sign of the zodiac represented by an inanimate object, they have to guard against coming across as aloof, cold, and metallic. Everything they do is all about artistic elegance, beauty, and pleasing others. Libras invariably have aesthetic qualities of such a high order that few can measure up. They are difficult to argue with, as they are suave and patently tactful. Diplomacy is their middle name.

AQUARIUS: THE WATER BEARER

Aquarius is the free-spirited, most unconventional sign of the zodiac. Aquarians are frequently ahead of the rest of us with ways to improve the world. They live in the future and prefer to break with the patterns of the past. An evolved Aquarian is a humanitarian, spiritually advanced, and a total groundbreaker. An unevolved Aquarian is the bohemian weirdo who refuses to do anything by the rules and does not fit in anywhere. Whether facing the higher version or the lower version, one can concur that all Aquarians are individualistic. There is a genius about them because they are so "out there" with their thoughts. They can get very committed to causes that frequently take them away from their families. These iconoclasts might do some crazy, outrageous things. The rest of us will look at them and think, "I wish I had the guts to live the way they do." Their symbol is the water bearer, but they are an air sign. Just this bit of confusion points to the fact that these complex individuals are often hard to explain. Instead of pouring water (emotions), they are pouring air (thoughts). Because they live inside the windmills of their minds, they are not the easiest sign to figure out, and like the wind, they are difficult to possess.

CANCER: THE CRAB

 Dreamy and emotional, Cancers often exhibit a tough exterior to cover up how incredibly soft and sensitive they are inside. Basically, if you get to know a Cancerian you will realize they are just plain mushy, though like their symbol, the crab, they try to protect their tender interior. Cancerians are sympathetic to a fault and easily moved to tears. It goes without saying that this can be a wonderful trait but also a difficult thing, as the joys and sorrows of the world affect them so deeply. They don't have much ability to deal with stress, so they tend to hide in their houses (think of a hermit crab ducking into his shell) or stay cloistered within themselves. Because they are so easily hurt, they rarely instigate a fight, but if you provoke them they will snap. It is rare, but the crab's pincers can hurt, but it is usually only done as a last resort when they are in self-preservation mode. These people are not fighters. Cancers are renowned for being domestic and nurturing. They are the types who will bring you milk and cookies if you are having a bad day. Crabs love to eat, and they will try to feed anyone they love.

SCORPIO: THE SCORPION

 It is not easy being a sign that is ruled by intensity. The scorpion is the shrewdest, deepest, and arguably the most powerful sign in the zodiac. These are the diggers, who are constantly searching for the meaning of life. They can be so obsessed with regeneration and transformation that they blow people out of a room with the sheer power of their need to explore the realms of human existence. Oftentimes, Scorpio doesn't know their own power. If you look closely at a Scorpio's circle of friends, you will find few in their inner circle. This is because they are incapable of doing anything on a superficial level. Everything has to have depth and meaning. If you don't go along with their fascination with big life-and-death issues, you might be left by the side of the road. Being a water sign, they are very emotional, sensitive beings, so they don't mean to hurt you. But like their symbol, the scorpion, they can sting you with their tail and then probably sting themselves in punishment for having hurt you. Loyalty and honor mean a lot to them. Scorpio will march with you into the deepest, darkest tunnels, and rejoice as you finally see light. However, if during your journey with Scorpio you ever betray their trust, they will never forgive you. There is no anger quite like a Scorpio's if they feel they have been treated unfairly. Scorpio's greatest assets are their determination and loyalty. As long as they appreciate that not everyone is going to be exactly like them, these are some of the most emotionally deep and loving people of the zodiac.

PISCES: THE FISH

The symbol for Pisces is two fish swimming in opposite directions, and therein lies the key to this zodiac sign. They can be one way one min-ute, and ten minutes later they are something else. Known as the chameleon of the zodiac, they are so sensitive that they read the energy from their surroundings and start to mimic whatever they are around. The dual qualities of their nature can sometimes produce an internal tug-of-war. They prefer to live in the world of dreams, fantasy, imagination, and en-chantment. If they get hooked into too much nonreality, they can become addicted personality types, always looking for the next thing to help them escape from the problems of the real world. Like all water signs, Pisceans are not naturally aggressive. They prefer to deal with life from a more spiritual point of view. A big part of their charm is their deep level of sympathy for others, coupled with an optimistic belief that a "happily ever after" is possible. They like to live in the realm of "what if." Some of the other signs might find them passive and ambivalent, but they need to understand that Pisces is so sensitive and naturally timid that they can get easily over-whelmed. They are deeply in touch with their feelings and can't be forced to do anything until they are good and ready.

. . .

A FULL ASTROLOGY chart has many aspects, all of which contribute to a complete picture of who you are and how you live in the world. This book focuses on communication styles as expressed by Mercury. Even if your Mercury placement does not match up blissfully with that of another person, it does not mean you can't have a productive relationship, whether that person is your sister, your boss, your friend, or your romantic partner. There could be compensating factors in the chart to make it all worthwhile in the end. The communication issue will always be there, however, so better to be forewarned. For the most part, people do not change, but awareness can help mitigate the intensity of any less-than-ideal Mercury pairing.

At one point in my life, for example, I was engaged to a man who seemed perfectly suited for me in many respects. He is a Pisces and I am a Cancer. According to most astrology books about relationships—almost all of which use sun signs to determine compatibility—we should have been a perfect match as we are both water signs.

However, there was a challenging aspect in our charts that we couldn't overcome: our Mercury signs were incompatible. My Mercury is in Cancer (a water sign) and his was in Sagittarius (a fire sign). When you put Mercury water and Mercury fire together, on the positive side it's possible there will be some playful banter as well as interesting conversations (because of opposite points of view). However, fire and water do not mix well in terms of day-to-day happiness.

Water is emotions: think of our watery tears. Fire is action and energy: think of our heart pumping as we heat up and sweat during a workout. Water wants to collect and hold. It wants to flow, like the rhythmic waves of the ocean or a moving river. When water gets angry, it floods and soaks; fire wants to explode, consume, and crackle. Fire can be aggressive but also warm and cozy when it is contained (think of the soothing qualities of a fireplace). But fire can also be harmful when it wants to eat up every tree in the forest, just as water can cause dangerous tidal waves of destruction. Water puts out fire. Fire heats up water and makes steam. One is not better than the other. It is just that certain combinations can be unsettling.

Fire Mercury placements make an individual direct, quick witted, and often sarcastic. Fire likes to ignite and doesn't mind a good blowup now and again. Water Mercury placements, by contrast, make for people who are generally soft spoken. Some might consider them conflict avoidant and too gentle with words; they rarely enjoy a "good" fight.

When I was with my partner, our communication styles prevented us from having a healthy relationship. His verbal fire energy packed too much heat for my softer way with words. I experienced his verbal style as cruel and his criticisms as an attack. He, in turn, felt that I was painfully oversensitive and way too emotional. He wondered why everything he said made me feel like I was being pierced by an arrow when he felt he was just expressing himself.

My goal is to help you make the best choice for peaceful coexistence with the people in your life. For example, in the love department, I want to spare you the pain of being matched with someone you can't communicate with on the most intimate level. Or let's say you have a daughter who drives you crazy because she doesn't seem to hear anything you say. If you look up her Mercury placement and compare it with yours, you may find that your styles are in conflict. If you know this, you can change your way of approaching her so that she can hear you. Or you may have a boss who is always critical of your work. That boss might have a fire sign Mercury, and you take every word she says to heart because your Mercury is in water. If you know your boss has a fire sign Mercury, you might stop and realize her style of speaking with you is just the way she is, and perhaps you can work with it better by not taking it so personally. With this book, you will be able to compare your Mercury sign with anyone else's Mercury sign. You will be able to easily find the descriptions of how you communicate together. You will also be able to discover if you, or the people you share your life with, were born during a Mercury retrograde period. This will further your understanding of their inner workings. Those born during Mercury retrograde are going to be open to more radical and visionary ideas. Their brains are wired to be a bit more unusual than those born during Mercury direct periods.

Knowing your Mercury compatibility is essential to your future happiness in the romance department. If you can't talk to your partner and feel heard, then when the going gets rough you will not feel as if you are with the right person. It won't matter how great the sex is or how compatible your sun signs are. At the end of the day, it's about whether you can communicate with your mate.

Of course, I want to stress that this book deals only with one aspect of a relationship: communication. Two people could have blissful moon connections, which is all about emotions, and that will bless the relationship with lots of easy compatibility even if the Mercury combination is less than ideal. Another point to keep in mind while reading these comparisons is that oftentimes Mercury is next to or in a geometric angle with another planet. When this occurs, it colors the way that Mercury placement will play out. It would be impossible to add that extra dimension of fine-tuning one's Mercury placement within the scope of this book. So keep in mind that only a complete astrological chart of your birth date, time, and place will provide a full picture of how Mercury will play out in your life. But for the purposes of this book, these Mercury combinations will give you an overall feeling of the key relationships in your life.

Use this book as a guide that enables you to see into people. This guide describes how two people will pair up on a mental level. It will tell you what to expect and how to work with it. You can get an understanding of your mental compatibility with your mother, father, boss, lover, child, sibling, and so on. Think of this book as a compass. These are like mini-horoscopes of every person you encounter. You are being given a snapshot of their communication style, which will help you better understand how to deal with the people in your life. I hope the planet Mercury speaks its truth to you, for more compassionate, understanding, and harmonious relationships.

3

THE GIFT OF MERCURY RETROGRADE

WHEN I WAS BORN, THE PLANET MERCURY WAS RE-trograde. This means at the exact moment of my birth, Mercury *appeared* to be moving backward in the sky, as seen by a human being standing on planet Earth. Mercury wasn't really doing anything other than continuing to travel in its normal orbital pathway around the sun. What actually happens when Mercury goes retrograde is that the planet slows in its orbit around the sun. The moment it is farthest from the sun is always the moment it is slowest. This gives earth, which normally orbits the sun more slowly than Mercury, the chance to catch up. What results is an optical illusion: as we pass Mercury, it appears to be going backward.

So what does all this mean? Why is it now so popular to mark Mercury retrograde periods in our calendars and believe that everything will be strange and unpredictable for a few weeks, several times a year? Why do so many astrologers turn into scaremongers and essentially recommend putting your life on hold during these periods? I believe that fear of Mercury retrograde originates in our historical misunderstanding of the "abnormality" we witness in the sky: our ancestors saw the motions of the heavens going out of sync and thought to themselves, "This can't be good." As with many things we perceive as different, we decided that different meant bad. I believe the idea that Mercury retrograde is a bad, dangerous time is so deeply ingrained in our beliefs now that people have come to expect bad things to happen during these weeks. Because of this common belief, people tend to have ominous feelings during Mercury retrograde. We anticipate problems. And of course if you look for problems, you will surely find them.

The word "retrograde" comes from the Latin *retrogradus*, which means going backward. This is in essence what Mercury retrograde periods feel like to us here on planet Earth—as if we are moving backward—regressing—and becoming disoriented. But is going backward necessarily a bad thing? When you are driving a car, aren't you thrilled that you have the option of putting your car into reverse? What if you only had forward motion as your way of moving? You could never get out of your garage or parallel park without this option. When we drive a manual transmission car, we need to press on the clutch and put the car in neutral before shifting to the next gear. When a car is in neutral, it means you don't have as much control and things can go wrong. That is exactly what Mercury retrograde can *feel* like. But if you look at these "neutral" periods of time as openings where things can naturally come together, then you have the possibility of something quite transformative. It is a healthy period where there is more open space between things, when pushing and pressing forward are not the way to go unless we want to "strip" our gears. You can't hit the brakes and the accelerator at the same time. We have to take turns with the depress cycle and the express cycle. Mercury retrograde wants to ask this question: "Will you give yourself a break? Can you stop trying to force everything?"

I believe we should take Mercury retrograde periods seriously, but I don't think we should use these times as an excuse for everything that is going wrong in our lives. It is my belief that we should watch for these Mercury retrograde periods and stay alert to them, just as we watch weather forecasts. It is useful to know when it is going to rain, so you can bring an umbrella. When Mercury goes retrograde, you can absolutely live your life as usual, despite all the scaremongering out there—you just need to be more mindful. It *is* safe to go on trips, start a new job, or sign a contract as long as you act with awareness. I believe this is good advice whether Mercury is retrograde or direct. Mark these retrograde periods on your calendar, but live from your gut and your intellect. We should never allow any planet to determine our movements one hundred percent. The planets are there to guide us, not admonish us. Astrology is meant to give us a deeper awareness of the patterns of the universe, so we can operate for the best within those patterns. Some patterns are easier than others to navigate, but none is inherently negative.

In fact, I see Mercury retrograde as a very special and positive time. Mercury retrograde asks us to slow down and return to source, or God, or our place of inner peace. Mercury retrograde's goal is to remind us that all sunshine all the time would make a desert. We need rain. If we choose not to heed Mercury retrograde's gentle reminder to slow down, to be mindful, then we may run into some issues when we fight what is. Mercury rules the nervous system, and these modern times have us all pretty wound up. Without the gift of these Mercury retrograde periods, we might not have the ability to readjust to a slower pace. It is like a built-in protection pattern to help humans remember that slowing down is a necessity in order to move forward skillfully and with awareness.

Since we live in such a high-RPM world, many of us are slaves to speed. Speed gets noticed. Speed gets praised. We are accustomed to instant communication. If someone doesn't respond to a text within a few minutes, we wonder why. Our lives are ruled by emails. We have to check and answer them daily, multiple times a day, or so many pile up that we get buried. Though Mercury is all about communication, emails and texts and instant messages don't afford us the deeper opportunity to learn someone's communication style. Mercury retrograde gives us the much-needed time to actually become aware of our different, individual styles of thinking and sharing information. It is a time to catch up with friends in real ways. Pick up the phone and *talk* with your friends. Or use snail mail and send a letter to someone. These are times to not make assumptions. Slow down, wait, and observe.

Unfortunately, going slow is anathema to life today. Everything is about going fast. Super-high-speed Internet access, overnight delivery services, "hot takes" on breaking news: the quicker the better. Rarely is anything revered for being slow. Speed can lead to a certain kind of immobility, though, a loss of connection, of creativity, of growth, because if you are going too fast, you will not notice anyone or anything that is not traveling at the same velocity. Human beings were designed to operate at foot speed, and yet it is rare to find people doing anything slowly. Fewer and fewer people are paying attention to the world around them and noticing the smaller, quieter things in life. Many of us have lost our connection to nature, which operates in both fast and slow cycles. Think of a bud waiting to bloom. We know a flower is in there, but if we pick at it, the bud will die. You can't force the flower to appear just because you know it is waiting to come out of that bud. Part of being human is to sit back and allow the natural rhythms of life to do what they need to do.

Most of us like speed. We don't like the slow. But everything cycles, and a great part of life is about loss and fading away; if we refuse to accept this, then we are not really living life in the healthiest way. The trick is to learn to be present and to live with a heightened awareness of what is around us. Mercury retrograde is about reminding us to be present to the slower cycles of life. A lot of revelations come out of silence and stillness. But most of us feel as if we have to always be engaged in something. Mercury retrograde is the down part of a cycle where an empty space appears. Once the space is emptied, it can be refilled when it goes into the Mercury direct cycle. We all need to be connected to something larger than ourselves. Mercury retrograde reminds us that many of us have exiled ourselves from the world of silence, contemplation, and meditation, and we need those parts of our existence to keep us in balance.

What if, instead of seeing Mercury retrograde as a time where communication goes haywire and our lives can go awry, we considered these periods as times of deep grace? A time when everything slows down and we can have a season of softness. Without these opposite periods in our lives, our days could become a monotonous hum. Music without space between notes is nothing but a mechanical buzzing. We need silence. I believe that during Mercury retrograde periods we are being handed the best time to let things come to us. Can you allow things to appear, rather than force things? Mercury retrograde has the power to heal us, if we can enjoy the art of allowing. To allow something means you are not forcing. This totally goes against our modern style, which is probably why people are so uncomfortable during Mercury retrograde. The invitation here is to reconsider all the amazing possibilities during Mercury retrograde. Relaxing, vacationing, daydreaming, playing— all of these are healthy things that many of us forget to do or choose not to do. When Mercury goes retrograde, it is a subtle reminder to go inward and remember what it felt like to go at a slower pace. The astrological symbol used to mark a retrograde planet is R_x —the same symbol that denotes a prescription in medicine. Perhaps it is time to look at these three-week Mercury retrograde periods as times when you are getting a much-needed prescription for your life: reflection and meditation.

So is Mercury retrograde a negative thing? I don't think so. And who is to say what is negative? If you look at a vulture soaring in the sky, it is a gorgeous thing to behold, though when it lands and you see its face, you might think, "Ugh, that is one ugly bird!" But the vulture's face is perfectly designed for its task, which is to consume animals that have died and by doing so support the natural cycles of our planet and the cycles of life itself. There is perfection in the design, just as there is perfection in the design of how the planets move. Like the vulture, Mercury retrograde periods might not always be pretty, but these periods are perfectly designed for what they were made to do, which is to slow us down. If you fight the weather, you will lose. Best to learn to enjoy these Mercury retrograde periods for what they are: gifts to help us find balance.

4

WHAT IF YOU WERE BORN DURING MERCURY RETROGRADE?

PEOPLE BORN DURING MERCURY RETROGRADE (LIKE myself) make up only 15–20 percent of the population, so we are definitely in the minority. Some astrologers believe that those born when Mercury is retrograde inherit, through the karmic process, a soul possessed of unusual awareness. Our brains are wired differently than those of other people. From my own experiences doing thousands of chart readings, I have found Mercury retrograde people to be highly perceptive, and they are often unconventional thinkers. Where Mercury retrograde resides inside the birth chart shows where that person's insights lie. For example, my Mercury retrograde is in the section of my chart that relates to dealing with large groups of people—which

I love doing when I teach my astrology workshops. In my experience, people born when Mercury is retrograde *are* often highly creative and innovative.

Though this aptitude for creative thought is a tremendous gift, being born in one of these periods comes with its own set of unique responsibilities, especially an imperative to really think before taking action. There is a constant need for Mercury retrograde people to slow down and reflect. They need to take care to heed their inner guidance system. This is true for all of us, but Mercury retrograde people can get into big trouble if they do not listen to that still, quiet inner voice. Remember, Mercury retrograde periods are times for reflection. So if you were born during Mercury retrograde, reflection periods are especially essential for your well-being.

Those few weeks each year when Mercury is retrograde are our time to shine. They're when we are most in our zone, feeling our groove. While everyone else seems to dread Mercury retrograde, we are best poised then to move full speed ahead to accomplish our goals. So while everyone else is complaining about how everything is going wrong, we get to relish the knowledge that this is our special small window of time to move forward. But this also means that when Mercury goes direct, we will feel the way everyone else does when it is retrograde. In other words, some might say we can't win. When we are in our zone, everyone else is out of their groove. When everyone else is moving forward, we are meant to spend more time in a reflective mode. That's a whole lot more time needing to be spent in an inward state than the rest of the population requires!

The impossibility of living strictly by the dictates of Mercury direct, which for me is much like Mercury retrograde, is the main reason I encourage all my clients not to fret over Mercury retrograde periods. If I got as worked up about Mercury direct periods as many people do about the retrograde periods, I would spend most of the year in a state of stress and anxiety. As I have mentioned many times, I never want a planet to determine my fate or my level of inner peace. It is up to me to be at peace with what is. Do I fight this constant need to slow down, breathe, and meditate? Absolutely! I am totally aware of how necessary this is for my mental health, but just as those of you born during Mercury direct often get a little impatient during Mercury retrograde, I can feel like this for most of the year if I allow it to get under my skin.

The best thing any of us can do, whether we were born when Mercury was retrograde or direct, is work with what is and accept the cosmic weather patterns. No matter what, we should live our lives by listening to our guts and heeding our inner voices. It is a far better way to make decisions than to make choices based on where a planet lies in its orbit. For example, if I listened to what most astrologers say about Mercury retrograde—that it is a time to avoid signing contracts, starting new relationships, or buying new equipment—I would be going against what is best for me. Conversely, even though retrograde periods are the best time for me to sign contracts and make big decisions, it certainly doesn't mean I can't sign a contract when Mercury is direct. That would be ridiculous, since most of the year Mercury is direct. I can't stop living my life while waiting for Mercury to return to its retrograde cycle.

And remember, except for the sun and the moon, all planets have periods of appearing to be retrograde. Yet we never caution people to avoid a new romantic relationship when Venus (the planet of love) appears to be going in reverse. Astrology can be dangerous if you come to believe you can't make a single move without consulting the stars and planetary placements. Astrology is a very complex study, and I believe all-or-nothing statements are deeply unhelpful.

It's true, my beliefs about Mercury retrograde definitely run counter to the majority of popular astrologers. But hey, my mind is designed to see the flip side of any situation—and I have Mercury retrograde to thank for that. With this book I want to empower everyone to see the reverse side of those typical arguments about the dangers of Mercury retrograde, and to see its gifts and powers instead.

5

HOW TO WORK WITH THESE MERCURY COMPARISONS

THIS IS THE PART OF THE BOOK WHERE YOU WILL BE able to learn more about your Mercury sign and those of the people in your life—and then compare the two! You could even look up the Mercury signs of people in other relationships—say, your parents or two of your colleagues—to better understand their dynamic.

To begin, please note that the signs are organized by their order in the zodiac:

♈ Aries	♌ Leo	♐ Sagittarius
♉ Taurus	♍ Virgo	♑ Capricorn
♊ Gemini	♎ Libra	♒ Aquarius
♋ Cancer	♏ Scorpio	♓ Pisces

As you move through the signs, you will notice that though each Mercury sign is described in full, there are fewer and fewer *combinations* described under each sign, to avoid repetitions. So Mercury Aries has descriptions for how each of the other eleven Mercury signs will combine with it, while Mercury Pisces has only one.

First look up your Mercury sign. Read the description of that Mercury sign's unique style of communication. Then look up the other person's Mercury sign and read the description for their placement. Once you have a basic knowledge of these two placements, you are ready to read what the combination of these two placements will feel like in your day-to-day life.

Let's take a few comparisons to see how this works.

Jason was born February 28, 1962. The planet Mercury was in the sign of Aquarius on that date. Jason's wife, Susan, was born May 1, 1965. The planet Mercury was in the sign of Aries.

After reading the descriptions for Mercury Aquarius and Mercury Aries, you would then read the description of the Mercury Aries / Mercury Aquarius combo, in the section on Mercury Aries. If you try to find this combo by looking for it under Mercury Aquarius, you will not see it there. This is because Aquarius is the second to the last zodiac sign, and the pairing was described already under Mercury Aries, the first zodiac sign.

Occasionally, a person is born just as Mercury is shifting between signs. For example, a woman born on August 11, 1940, arrived in this world just as Mercury was moving from Cancer to Leo. To determine her true Mercury sign, you would need to know her time of birth. Given this, you have two choices when looking up a birth date that falls as Mercury changed signs. You can read the description for both and get a sense of which feels more accurate. Or use the Mercury calculator at www.lunarium.co.uk/moonsign/ mercury.jsp and enter the birth date, time, and place of birth to learn the exact Mercury placement. For example, if this woman was born at 6 P.M. in New York City, her Mercury placement would be Leo.

MERCURY SIGN COMBINATIONS

MERCURY ARIES

A PERSON WITH A MERCURY PLACEMENT IN FIERY Aries will be direct, blunt, and very likely to let verbal sparks fly when upset. They are blessed with quick minds, yet impatient tongues. It is the essential nature of Mercury Aries to be superfast to tell it like it is (from their viewpoint, of course!). Their verbal style is likely to have a competitive edge. Their ability to think on their feet is impressive. Most of their quick decisions are accurate, but they must realize that no one is one hundred percent correct all the time. Mercury Aries is able to speak up when they passionately believe in something, which is the positive usage of this placement. They have little problem standing in their truth. However, they can be swift to complain when they don't get what they want. They are likely to just as quickly forget about what they said and move on. It is not that they are short-tempered or rude; it is just that their minds move speedily from one context to the next. They like to put forward their opinions, some of which have not gone through a filtration process. As a raconteur, Mercury Aries can switch topics better than anyone. However, they can just as easily lose their concentration, and they tend to buckle under the strain of anything that is repetitive or forced. The sign of Aries has a pioneering quality, so when Mercury is in this sign, their minds are clearly more adventurous when it comes to pursuing intellectual activities. Because they are so open to new theories and thoughts, others can value Mercury Aries for their active and responsive ways of thinking; however, these same qualities can also be a detriment in that they are sometimes fearless to a fault. Consciously taking the time to slow down, notice social cues, and truly understand that their words have an effect on others would be helpful for Mercury Aries. Often people with Mercury Aries have a sarcastic sense of humor and love to tease. Being playful in their basic nature, Mercury Aries enjoys people who can match their quick wit. They appreciate folks who easily handle what they dish out and who do not take things too personally. At the end of the day, Mercury Aries prefers to get right to the point and march on to the next topic of conversation.

MERCURY ARIES COMBINATIONS

Mercury Aries / Mercury Aries

♈ ♈

Two red-hot energies—fire and fire—combine in this duo. A pair of Mercury Aries will enjoy the challenge of an occasional verbal sparring contest. Both are direct and sometimes brutally honest. They may exchange roles; one person may play the aggressor on one day and then the peacemaker the next. There is a competitive energy between these two. Sometimes they cross the line into cruelty, but both seem to inherently understand that they don't mean to be cruel. Most of the time there is simply a playful and sassy energy to their conversations. There is nothing halfway about these two. They will have periodic volcanic blowups that are usually well intentioned, but if they are not careful, their discussions can lead to flat-out verbal warfare. You do not want to be around when these two are both in a bad mood. Their fights are legendary, and once words are spoken, it is hard to take them back.

Mercury Aries / Mercury Taurus

♈ ♉

The nature of Mercury Aries is to push an agenda using words that may feel aggressive to the softer Mercury Taurus. Mercury Aries is a fire sign, and Mercury Taurus is an earth sign. It is the nature of fire to continually seek something to consume, just as a forest fire burns the trees. Unfortunately, the Mercury Taurus person may feel as if they are being burnt to a crisp by Mercury Aries's occasional verbal tirades. However, Mercury Aries doesn't mean to be difficult. They are just very "to the point," and this can feel pushy and cruel to Mercury Taurus. When Mercury Taurus has had enough, they will dump a big pile of earth on that Mercury Aries fire and put it right out. Mercury Taurus will do this by standing firm. They will not budge, no matter what Mercury Aries says. Eventually Mercury Aries will get tired of being unable to light a match to the recalcitrant Mercury Taurus. But Mercury Aries will most likely try to save a few smoldering ashes, and will ignite another fire soon enough. Mercury Taurus only speaks after thinking things through, while Mercury Aries will just let it rip. How can these two very different styles of communication ever be reconciled? With this pairing, Mercury Taurus will need to learn how to forgive and to realize that the Mercury

Aries person is prone to verbal volatility. The trick is to re-member that turbulent conversations are not an everyday occurrence. In fact, most of the time, Mercury Taurus can sit back and enjoy the irresistible magnetism and good hu-mor of Mercury Aries.

Mercury Aries / Mercury Gemini

♈ ♊

Mercury Gemini loves intellectual pursuits, wordplay, and language. Mercury Gemini people are very curious, and they seek to increase their knowledge about all subjects that pique their curiosity. Since Aries is the sign associated with the head, there is an interesting compatibility here. Mercury Aries encourages Mercury Gemini to engage in anything that expands the brain, and they love to push each other forward to learn more and more. The only danger with this pairing is that the verbal passion of Mercury Aries may start to feel like domination to the more airy and detached Mercury Gemini way of thinking. Mercury Aries always wants to have the last word. If these two get into a verbal disagreement, their shared love for intense, mentally stimulating conversations will hopefully lessen Mercury Gemini's irritation with Mercury Aries's need to win. This can be an interesting and vital combination, as long as both focus on how much fun they have talking about what they are passionate about. Mercury Gemini will probably learn to detach when Mercury Aries gets too intense. Neither should take this as a negative aspect to their relationship; it is just the way this pairing ebbs and flows.

Mercury Aries / Mercury Cancer

♈ ♋

Mercury Aries is an aggressive placement. They use words to either fight for what they believe in or fight just for the sake of having a "good" fight. Mercury Cancer may respond to this behavior by shutting down verbally. Mercury Cancer has a hard time speaking up and defending its position. Just like a crab that retreats to its hole, Mercury Cancer will do anything to avoid a verbal conflict. On a happier note, Mercury Aries will have no problem making a verbal stand and fighting for Mercury Cancer if need be. Mercury Aries is a fire sign and Mercury Cancer is a water sign. Fire and water are not easy elements to blend. However, the two individuals should consider how fire and water sometimes do blend well together. Think about the pleasure of heated water in a bathtub or the enjoyment of a hot cup of tea. Perhaps Mercury Aries will learn how to be more verbally sensitive from watching how Mercury Cancer wins people over using gentle language. And maybe Mercury Cancer will learn from Mercury Aries how to avoid being pushed around.

♈ ♌

Mercury Aries and Mercury Leo can be a verbally passionate combination. Directness is the operative word for Mercury Aries, and they love that same quality of speech in others. Mercury Leo has a magnanimous spirit, which matches Mercury Aries's enthusiasm. In this combination, Mercury Aries should abandon any attempt to verbally dominate Mercury Leo; Mercury Leo will never play second fiddle. However, if you give them what they want (which is lavish praise), they will be purring at your feet. The quick-witted Mercury Aries is skillful at delivering lots of compliments. In return, the Mercury Leo will praise them and repeatedly tell them how wonderful they are. This pairing can appear to be a mutual admiration society. There is a nice back-and-forth energy between these two. They revitalize each other in an enthusiastic way. Both parties appreciate one another's warm and spontaneous communication styles. Their sense of humor is similar, which makes for fun times. Both approach intellectual topics with equal vigor. There is never any wondering about what the other is thinking, because they tell it like it is. There is a healthy synergy here. However, you would not want the hotel room next door when these two get into a fight. A small discussion can turn into a heated one. If they both are not careful, there could be a nuclear verbal explosion.

Mercury Aries / Mercury Virgo

♈ ♍

Mercury Aries with Mercury Virgo is a tricky combination, which can only work if both individuals are super-tolerant of one another's style of communication. Mercury Virgo is meticulous with words. They will take a complicated subject and distill the essence of their thoughts into a concise package. They like people's thought processes to be realistic, grounded, and sane. Of course, few people (except another Mercury Virgo) can measure up to their exacting standards when it comes to their demand for rational thinking. Mercury Aries is quick to share their viewpoint, and they rarely stop to think before they blurt out their opinion. Mercury Virgo is just the opposite. Thankfully, Virgo is a pretty patient sign. Mercury Virgo might be able to put up with that blistering-fast Mercury Aries tongue, but only if the outbursts are few and far between. Tolerance is key for these two.

Mercury Aries / Mercury Libra

♈ ♎

Aries and Libra are natural counterparts. Fire meets air. As in nature, you can't have a fire without oxygen. There is a symbiotic relationship between these two. Mercury Libra is very diplomatic and has a heightened sense of fairness. They are skillful at charming people with their words and use language to create harmony. Sometimes they can almost be too particular with words. They might be critical of the sometimes rough and primitive communication style of Mercury Aries. There is a youthful energy to Mercury Aries's choice of words, and sometimes (just like a youth) they speak before thinking. Why would Libra be interested in Mercury Aries? Because Mercury Libra doesn't mind holding space for the wild Mercury Aries, whose free imagination fascinates them. Mercury Libra provides a comforting outlet for Mercury Aries to express all their fiery thoughts, which they deeply appreciate. It is a vital combination that, for the most part, blends powerfully.

Mercury Aries / Mercury Scorpio

♈ ♏

Mercury Aries and Mercury Scorpio pack a powerful punch. They are both equally strong in their opinions, and therein lies the problem. They have very different ways of developing and expressing ideas. Mercury Aries is a very outward sign. Mercury Scorpio is the most internal of all the zodiac signs. Mercury Aries will let everyone know exactly how they feel, while Mercury Scorpio will let very few know their feelings. Mercury Scorpio wants to dig for the truth and is obsessed with figuring things out. Mercury Aries generally does not have an obsession with hidden meanings and deeper truths. They take things as they come and move on. Mercury Scorpio needs to get to the bottom of everything, and their mind will hold on to thoughts for a very long time. But Mercury Aries is not that interested in analyzing everything. Therefore, Mercury Scorpio's passion for overanalyzing may drive Mercury Aries crazy. This is not an easy alliance. In this pairing, both individuals would have to work hard to not criticize each other's style of processing thoughts. If they are not tolerant, this combination can have incendiary results. The trick is to accept their very different styles and learn to appreciate that if they were exactly the same it would be redundant and boring. And neither of these signs wants to be bored!

Mercury Aries / Mercury Sagittarius

There is a strong potential for synergy and great communication when the fire of Aries meets the fire of Sagittarius. These two both revel in passionate, often heated, discussions. Usually they consider their conversations to be scintillating. Both can be impetuous, impulsive, and quick with their opinions, however. Neither has much of a filter when it comes to speaking their minds. In fact, they thrive on having a "good" argument once in a while. Since both are from the fire element, they can spew words that carry a lot of heat. To an outsider, it may seem like this pair enjoys firing off peppery words on a regular basis. Each one's passion for speaking with fervor is matched by the other, so onlookers might find them argumentative. Nevertheless, this dynamic works for them. As the saying goes, "If you can't take the heat, get out of the kitchen." Well, these two firecrackers love the kitchen!

Mercury Aries / Mercury Capricorn

♈ ♑

Oh boy, this can be a tough one. Imagine a ten-year-old boy (Mercury Aries) getting into an argument with Grandpa (Mercury Capricorn). Mercury Aries will get frustrated when Mercury Capricorn is pokey and usually so serious. Mercury Capricorn will be critical of the constant verbal pushiness from Mercury Aries. Mercury Aries won't give up, trying hard to impart their truths to the steadfast Mercury Capricorn. Mercury Capricorn believes nothing is true unless it has stood the test of time. But Mercury Aries could not care less about the test of time and instead believes what they believe in the moment. Mercury Capricorn picks words with careful deliberation. It is as if there is a drill sergeant living in their brain, and every word comes out only after inspection. The only way this pairing can work is if Mercury Aries stops reminding Mercury Capricorn that they sometimes feel like a stick-in-the-mud. And then Mercury Capricorn needs to be willing to accept that Mercury Aries's youthful exuberance with words is just that—youthful, and not always meant to be cruel. In fact, they both could stand to learn from the other. The great thing about this pairing is that despite all their differences, they enjoy each other's sense of humor. Mercury Capricorn has a dry wit, and Mercury Aries eats it up and thrives on their playful banter.

Mercury Aries / Mercury Aquarius

♈ ♒

Mercury Aries and Mercury Aquarius will never run out of things to talk about. The fire of Aries meets the expansive air of Aquarius. Fire can't exist without air. This pair knows how to spur one another on. They have a nice, expansive way of combining thoughts, and their conversations flow naturally and freely. They will have no trouble communicating, and in fact, it may seem as if they can read each other's minds. Having this kind of mental compatibility is a big blessing. Mercury Aries has a spirited way of engaging the big-picture perspective of Mercury Aquarius, who loves to communicate with everyone. They both enjoy mental activities that increase their curious natures. These two spark each other's imagination. Mercury Aquarius has no problem dealing with the impetuous tongue on Mercury Aries. And Mercury Aries delights in the space that the airy Mercury Aquarius provides.

♈ ♓

This is a challenging combination for effective communication and positive relationships. Mercury Pisces feels everything, and the verbal tirades that can occasionally come out of Mercury Aries's mouth can cut to the core. Mercury Aries will unknowingly ride roughshod over the delicate Mercury Pisces. Mercury Pisces would have to be very thick-skinned to withstand Mercury Aries's directness. Sometimes, Mercury Aries can be a nice instigator to Mercury Pisces, by encouraging them to speak up regarding whatever is bothering them. Mercury Pisces tends to be a bit wishy-washy in the verbal department, as they have a tendency to not speak up and often withhold words until they feel safe. If Mercury Aries is too short fused, ultrasensitive Mercury Pisces might lose their sense of safety and retreat into the corner and go silent. This will drive Mercury Aries mad! If they both lose their sense of balance, this will not be a recipe for intellectual compatibility. If Mercury Aries can accept and enjoy the softness of Mercury Pisces, without trying to convert them, this can work. And Mercury Pisces should work on realizing that the passion behind Mercury Aries's words just shows how much they care.

MERCURY TAURUS

MERCURY TAURUS IS A PRACTICAL THINKER. THEY do not put up with a lot of nonsense. "Say what you mean, and mean what you say!" is their motto. They prefer honest, calm discussions. It drives them nuts when others digress during a conversation; Mercury Taurus is efficient with words and likes every conversation to have a purpose. Common sense comes naturally to them. Taurus is symbolized by the bull, an animal of great, silent power. When you put Mercury in this sign, it can make the individual stubborn about certain thoughts. They can dig in their heels and are sometimes unyielding. These individuals tend to be steadfast; they are usually considerate and prefer to use calming words. During an argument, Mercury Taurus excels at doggedly stating their case and will often wear people down with their persistence, which to other Mercury signs can seem like intractability. There is nothing overtly aggressive about their method of communicating, but they are certainly determined to get their points across. With amazing powers of concentration, these are the folks who also can retain copious amounts of information and whip out evidence from their memory files at just the right moment. They do not like to be pushed into making decisions before they are good and ready. A Mercury Taurus person needs to spend considerable time contemplating all of their options. Their fixed opinions feel heartfelt and genuine to some but pig-headed to others. There is nothing zippy about their communication style. Their brains operate at a methodical pace that works for them but can be frustrating for some of the more fiery Mercury placements, like Mercury Aries, Leo, and Sagittarius, who will want to say, "Just spit it out!" Mercury Taurus minds have a tendency to block out things that they don't want to hear, as well as to fixate on certain thoughts, which can become obsessive. Never in a rush and rarely verbally angry, Mercury Taurus people are usually quite stable. Their methodical minds are grounded in dealing with what is evident to them, and they are not known for jumping to conclusions.

MERCURY TAURUS COMBINATIONS

♉ ♉

This is a highly compatible combination in which two people may feel as if they live inside a magic bubble where their similar thinking styles bring a great deal of comfort. Both are likely to agree on matters of taste, whether in terms of food, books, or decorating. Their minds and senses are especially in alignment when it comes to earthly matters, including money. Coins are made of metals found in the earth, and bills are made of paper, which comes from trees, and earthly financial issues are where these two tend to focus a lot of their mental energies. Very practical and somewhat plodding in nature, Mercury Taurus people rarely get into spats. Their inherently stubborn natures would rather wait out any verbal storm rather than enter the fray. Preferring quiet atmospheres, these two are happiest not wasting verbal energy and speaking only when they have something to say. When Mercury Taurus meets Mercury Taurus, they instinctively recognize nearly every mood and attitude. There is a calm acceptance of each other and a relaxed way of sharing thoughts and feelings. It is almost as if the hullabaloo of the outside world doesn't have much chance of upsetting their combined mental compatibility.

Mercury Taurus / Mercury Gemini

♉ ♊

If Mercury Taurus and Mercury Gemini were in a museum together, Mercury Gemini would be reading all the little signs under each painting, chatting about what they think about each one, while Mercury Taurus would be silently nodding. Mercury Taurus would only share their thoughts with Mercury Gemini if they felt their thoughts had practical application or worth. At first, Mercury Taurus will enjoy Mercury Gemini's curiosity about the who, what, why, and where of everything. However, with time, this combination can become exhausting because Mercury Gemini is basically obsessed with novelty, while Mercury Taurus is obstinate and resists change. This pairing can work if Mercury Gemini accepts that Mercury Taurus is a lot slower to make up their mind. But the good thing about the Mercury Taurus way of thinking is that when they make up their mind, they are usually unshakable, and Mercury Gemini can take great comfort in that type of solid thinking. Mercury Gemini wants to constantly expand their knowledge base. Due to their restless minds, they tend to abhor anything that is routine. Mercury Taurus, however, does not have a restless mind. Their goal is to achieve mental stability, and they enjoy a good deal of structure. They enjoy routines. Sometimes, Mercury Taurus can allow themselves to enjoy the "exotic" freshness of Mercury Gemini's expansive outlook. However, these two have to be careful about getting frustrated with one another. The challenge here is for Mercury Gemini to spur Mercury Taurus to develop a more expansive view of various topics without criticizing them for being so attached to their practical and grounded mental viewpoints.

Mercury Taurus / Mercury Cancer

♉ ♋

Mercury Taurus and Mercury Cancer communicate with such ease that others will be able to sense their mental synergy and marvel at their similarities. Both dislike arguing and instead prefer having a sense of stability with everyone with whom they interact. Both would rather not deal with people who use words as weapons, and both are sensitive to language—especially to tones of voice. Mercury Taurus and Mercury Cancer are excellent listeners and can almost intuitively sense what the other is trying to express. They are likely to be gentle in their methods to get the other to open up. Mercury Cancer is influenced by emotions. Mercury Taurus is skillful at holding space for a distraught Mercury Cancer, who lives in the watery realm of easily flowing tears. Both thrive on being reasonable, and neither likes to be hurried or harried. There is a lovely mental receptivity between these two, and at times they can seem perfectly balanced. The only caution here is that water and earth can make mud, so they need to guard against becoming mentally gloomy.

♉ ♌

Here we enter the realm of fire meeting earth. Mercury Leo (fire) is verbally expansive, and Mercury Taurus (earth) is verbally contained. Fire sign Mercury placements are psychologically able to let go. Earth sign Mercury placements are naturally retentive. Mercury Leo is all about passion. They can spin a tale with lots of linguistic fireworks. In conversation, they are the types to blurt out what they passionately care about, using words like "stupendous," "awesome," and "absolutely." In their speech, it is all-or-nothing. Both Mercury Leo and Mercury Taurus have strong opinions, but Mercury Leo is more likely to express them. A Mercury Taurus speaks with a kind of plodding practicality, which can feel very good when you want to restore confidence or order. With Mercury Taurus, there isn't a lot of hyperbole. Mercury Leo is lavish with words and praise. Mercury Taurus is not likely to go overboard in the sentimentality department. The fundamental qualities of these two are not in tandem. Rather than giving up on each other for either being too dramatic (Leo) or too pokey (Taurus), they would be better off appreciating the way they can merge their two styles into something quite special. The stalwart Mercury Taurus can beautifully hold the pizzazz of Mercury Leo. However, if they start rumbling about how the other shares feelings and thoughts, they might feel disconnected from each other. If Mercury Taurus can learn to enjoy the spontaneous way Mercury Leo sparks things up, this can work. Meanwhile, Mercury Leo could stand to remember how nice it is to be with someone who is richly present. Balance is always a possibility with these too, as long as both individuals are conscious of their differences.

ŏ ♍

The intellect, which involves memory and perception, helps us make inferences about ourselves and the world around us. When two similar intellectual energies, like Mercury Taurus and Mercury Virgo (both earth placements), join together, there is a tremendous sense of being with someone who originates from the same mental sphere of influence. Both individuals will feel like they share a high percentage of similar inner observations, and this can feel decidedly pleasant. The twelve different Mercury sign placements vary tremendously in the intensity and rhythm of how they communicate; yet these two present their thoughts in a very similar and straightforward manner. There is a flow here and a nourishing sense of peace. Neither sign is known for being overly emotional with words, but they both sense things deeply and can be moved by simple aesthetic pleasures like the color of a rose or the architecture of a building. It is just that the whole realm of words and language is very subtle for them. For both, this Mercury placement is about inner thinking first, before expression. Mercury Virgo is capable of seeing the big picture as well as the smallest detail. It's as if they have a built-in lens inside their brain that allows the picture to change in size.

Therefore, they look at things with a wide viewpoint and then are able to distill the essence of a situation with concise language. Mercury Taurus enjoys this because they interpret this quality as precision—something they admire, especially when it comes to words. Virgo is the perfectionist of the zodiac, which fits this placement since it requires that everything be "just so." Overall, there is a feeling of intellectual harmony between these two Mercury signs.

Mercury Taurus / Mercury Libra

♉ ♎

In this pairing we have two people who like things to be verbally cool, calm, and collected. Mercury Taurus knows how to speak in a way that is clear and pragmatic. Mercury Libra is the consummate elegant communicator, who can be direct and strong but usually in a polite way. There is usually quite a dry wit to Mercury Libra's sense of humor. They are a master in the art of nuances, and they like to indulge in clever banter. For Mercury Libra, everything is about partnership. A great conversation for them is one that feels like a tennis match. Mercury Taurus enjoys the back-and-forth rallies and the infinite complexities of the Mercury Libra mind. Mercury Libra is a lot less emotional than Mercury Taurus. Sometimes Mercury Taurus can feel as if Mercury Libra is a little too coolheaded for their taste, but overall there is a symmetry of thought between these two.

Mercury Taurus / Mercury Scorpio

♉ ♏

These two get along well until they don't! Mercury Taurus (earth) meets Mercury Scorpio (water), and as in Nature, for the most part, there is a lovely blending here, just as the earth holds a lake and contains it. However, if the water rises and the lake floods, it is no longer so bucolic. Of all the Mercury placements, those in Mercury Scorpio are the most secretive, but every so often they let loose with a fierceness that is laced with a lot of emotion and passion. Mercury Scorpio can be the hardest for others to truly know, because they keep a lot of their thoughts hidden in a subterranean vault. As a result, they can unintentionally seem secretive and therefore not entirely trustworthy. They will eventually share the deep feelings and ideas that swirl around in their probing minds, but only if you have proven to be safe. Mercury Scorpio is always waiting for the other shoe to drop. Ironically, Mercury Taurus hardly ever drops a shoe, so in fact they are well suited for each other since Mercury Taurus can supply just the right words to help Mercury Scorpio feel secure. But Mercury Scorpio is highly suspicious, and trust is a big issue for them. It is important that Mercury Taurus never intentionally aggravate Mercury Scorpio into speaking before they are ready.

If Mercury Taurus can just hold space and be patient with Mercury Scorpio, this can be a lovely combination. Mercury Scorpio has a bit of a rascally sense of humor. And Mercury Taurus can have a lot of laughs with Mercury Scorpio, as long as they are not the target of some of Mercury Scorpio's biting yet humorous jabs. These jabs don't come too often, but when they do, Mercury Taurus should learn not to take them personally. There is something compelling about this combination in that it is a bit like a cat-and-mouse chase. They are quite fascinated with each other, and the quality of their conversations is often unforgettable.

Mercury Sagittarius (fire) can be quite brilliant at times, but sometimes their quick-fire thoughts are not backed up by firsthand experience. The rapidity of their ideas is impressive, but sometimes they lack the requisite follow-through to turn these ideas into something concrete. When they are on a roll with a concept they are developing, they will surge ahead with such force that others may be left in the dust. Oftentimes it is the more practical Mercury earth placements (Taurus, Virgo, Capricorn) who supply structure to the extremely changeable Mercury Sagittarius. It's inevitable that, due to their slower mental pace, Mercury Taurus will feel as if they are plodding along miles behind Mercury Sagittarius. Mercury Taurus looks before they leap, and their ideas are always substantiated. Mercury Sagittarius is an impulsive placement; Mercury Taurus is cautious, and therein lies the main difficulty between these two. Problems may arise when Mercury Sagittarius tries to force Mercury Taurus to think faster and match their pace. Mercury Sagittarius tends to get impatient when others can't keep up with their quick processing abilities. However, they need to realize that going fast can mean missing out on some important details. For short-term interactions, this pairing can be an enjoyable combination. Mercury Taurus can thoroughly enjoy the freedom of Mercury Sagittarius as it speeds along the mental highways of life. But long term, these two may run into troubles due to the very different paces with which they process thoughts and communicate.

Mercury Taurus / Mercury Capricorn

♉ ♑

Here two similar spirits meet. Both Mercury Taurus and Mercury Capricorn are pragmatic, commonsensical-thinking individuals. They will be highly supportive of one another, and if in a working relationship, they could certainly build an empire. Much of their conversations involve their mutual passion for building something, whether it be an architectural monument, a family, or a company. However, these two place such a strong emphasis on practicality that they can sometimes get into mental ruts. They make a good match in many types of relationships both at home and at work, unless they get stuck inside a boring loop where they forget to spark things up. Overall, they blend remarkably well, but Mercury Taurus should never take Mercury Capricorn for granted. Mercury Capricorn is serious, hard-working, and sometimes forgets to acknowledge that they need downtime, too. Mercury Taurus is perfectly capable of reminding Mercury Capricorn that they do not need to be the responsible leader of every situation. Once in a while, Mercury Capricorn needs to be relieved from the duty of being the decision maker. In which case, Mercury Taurus is very capable of filling in. These two just need to work on allowing their inner child to take over once in a while.

Mercury Aquarius can get so caught up in larger-than-life intellectual concepts that they fail to notice Mercury Taurus has completely fallen asleep. These two are both gentle with words, but they process thoughts in totally different manners. Mercury Aquarius is all about being neutral and open to all possibilities. They are the type of thinkers who are often completely ingenious, with many leading-edge thoughts roaming around in their heads. Mercury Taurus appreciates these mental gymnastics, but they can feel as if they are separated by the wide gulf known as reality. Mercury Aquarius loves to soak in the world of "what if?" and Mercury Taurus prefers to consider "what now?" This basic difference in their conceptual viewpoints doesn't have to be a bad thing. Each can bring what the other needs. For example, Mercury Aquarius could use the practical groundedness of Mercury Taurus to anchor their ideas into actionable steps. Meanwhile, Mercury Taurus will realize the imaginative freedom of Mercury Aquarius opens them up to the great benefits of expansive thoughts and imaginative play.

♉ ♓

Mercury Pisces has a mind that absorbs information through all the senses. They educate themselves through the filter of inner emotions. They are feeling people who believe that true intimacy involves sharing a whole myriad of emotional expressions. For the most part, Mercury Taurus can enjoy this, but it will occasionally become too much, as Mercury Taurus is much less sentimental. Mercury Taurus is concrete, whereas Mercury Pisces can be exasperatingly vague, which can drive Mercury Taurus batty. Just as a nice rainfall can water the plants, one has to consider that too much water—that is, emotions (Pisces)—can cause a huge downpour and flood the earth (Taurus). At an intellectual level, there is a symbiotic flow between these two, which can be interrupted if Mercury Pisces sometimes can't stop flowing through the emotional outpouring of too many words. which will make Mercury Taurus want to retreat. Despite these differences, this combination tends to be pleasant and easygoing because elementally they are compatible. Occasionally minor adjustments will be necessary, but overall, these two signs are comfortable with one another's style of communicating. There is an intuitive knowingness between these two. To an outsider, it might seem as if Mercury Taurus does more of the heavy lifting. But Mercury Taurus doesn't mind being a steady anchor to the ocean-dwelling Mercury Pisces, who could use some mental grounding.

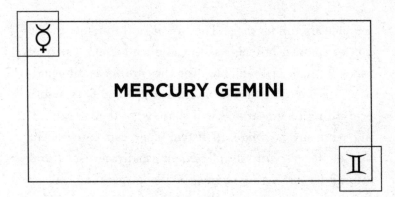

MERCURY GEMINI

MERCURY IS THE PLANET THAT RULES GEMINI. THIS means the planet Mercury is most at home in the sign of Gemini. Since Mercury is all about communication, Mercury Gemini people tend to be supercommunicators: it's like they have double the Mercury energy. Intellectual stimulation is a necessity for these people, as they tend to be extremely curious. As children, they are often the ones asking adults why things are the way they are. Mercury Gemini people are questioners. They have a deep thirst for information about a variety of topics and like to gather information. Often they are excellent teachers, especially of languages and literature. Words are their deck of cards, and they like to play games with them. Crossword puzzles and scrabble are fun for them. They are logical thinkers and do not let emotion influence their judgment. Their clarity of thought can be brilliant; however, they are not sentimentalists. This is a mind that operates like a sponge. They absorb everything they hear and will share what they are thinking with anyone who will listen. They can be excellent mimics. People with this placement usually have a natural affinity for picking up languages. Being sparkling conversationalists, they can tap-dance with words. They weave stories and anecdotes with ease. Fast talkers and quick witted, these folks are often a few steps ahead of the rest of us. But because making charming conversation comes so easily to them, they can sometimes be a bit glib. Mercury in Gemini loves ideas and plans but is not so tethered to the earthly reality of getting things done, so the challenge for a Mercury Gemini is to actually see tasks through rather than just talk about them. And that's the main thing with Mercury Geminis: they love to talk! They love to hold forth at length on almost any subject and can lose sight of boundaries when it comes to sharing their thoughts. They could be accused of unbridled communication. Their brain is like a scanner, noticing patterns and sequences and looking for things that are out of sync with a logical order. They think about talking and they talk about thinking. Round and round they go, like swirling breezes, either captivating their audiences or wearing them down with words. Overall, however, this is an especially strong placement for Mercury, and people with Mercury Gemini are lucky to have been born with such a sharp mind and a quick wit. They have a knack for seeing things as they are, without allowing emotional considerations to cloud their judgment.

MERCURY GEMINI COMBINATIONS

♊ ♊

The symbol of Gemini is the twins. So when you put two Geminis together, it is like a meeting of four minds, rather than two. On the plus side, this pairing brings with it infinite inquisitiveness as both people in this pair have ravenous minds and are willing to try almost anything. That said, with double the intellectual curiosity and verbal prowess, there can be *a lot* of noise between them. At times, the two might be bandying about so many words that their meanings get lost in the cacophony. In the midst of this, they might have difficulty seeing and hearing each other clearly because of the sheer volume of words. To outsiders their conversations might seem extremely verbose, but each feels happy with the flow of words, and they are inextricably connected to the other, to the point that it is difficult to separate them. They can both speak expertly about many topics. Each person in this pairing should try to cultivate a concise and cogent way of getting their points across, rather than rambling on and on. Perhaps sometimes it would be wise for each to consider how many times their inquiring minds have perhaps become a little neurotic. At its best, this is a meaningful combination of two like-minded people whose intellectual curiosity generates great ideas—both just need to guard against the verbosity that can make their communication feel like walking into a verbal hall of mirrors.

♊   ♋

Mercury Gemini loves wordplay and battles of wit. Though Mercury Cancer enjoys Mercury Gemini's questioning and quick mind, they have to guard against being hurt because Mercury Cancer is highly sensitive and supersentimental. As a result, if the conversation moves into the realm of teasing that Mercury Gemini sometimes enjoys, Mercury Cancer may have a hard time handling it, even if the banter is good-natured. This can be difficult for Mercury Gemini, who ideally hopes for a partner—at home, at work, or socially—who can "keep up." Cancer is a water sign, so a Mercury placement here leads to an emotional communication style—not just in how Mercury Cancer speaks, but also in how they perceive another's words. They may hear Mercury Gemini's light-hearted teasing as mean-spirited; like a sponge, they will absorb and retain any and all words that Mercury Gemini uses, holding on to these "slights" in their minds. This may lead to periods of stalled communication, as Mercury Cancer withdraws in the face of Mercury Gemini's more emotionally detached style. For their communication to be positive and productive, Mercury Cancer will have to practice not taking things quite so personally, and Mercury Gemini will have to remember and accept that empathy is a valuable skill in communicating. Mercury Cancer is a sentimentalist. Mercury Gemini is not.

Mercury Gemini / Mercury Leo

♊ ♌

Mercury Gemini's insatiable curiosity and hungry mind mean they love reading, going to bookstores, hearing authors speak, attending the theater, seeing movies, going to concerts, and the like. Mercury Leo loves to be out in the world, front and center, so these two make for good company. And while Mercury Leo's natural vivacity supports Mercury Gemini's inquisitiveness, Mercury Gemini's way with words is the perfect foil for Mercury Leo's love of being the center of attention. Mercury Gemini is especially adept at providing the verbal flattery Mercury Leo requires. Mercury Leo *loves* the way Mercury Gemini uses words: so charming and quick-witted. And Mercury Gemini loves that Mercury Leo can keep up with their verbal pace. But they share less desirable qualities, too, related to their mutual quickness: neither is particularly patient, and both have little tolerance for people who take too long to get to the point, are not clear speakers, are "overly" emotional (as they see it), or who are still talking about some issue they both feel should have been dropped long before. This can mean that Mercury Leo and Mercury Gemini may have difficulty truly hearing each other in an argument or communicating effectively when tempers run high. Between the two of them, Mercury Gemini tends to be the more verbose, and their lengthy verbal outpourings can try Mercury Leo. But as long as Mercury Gemini remembers to pepper their patois with lots of flattery for their lion counterpart, and as long as Mercury Leo stimulates the curiosity of the Mercury Gemini instead of concentrating on the spotlight, there is a natural affinity between them.

♊ ♍

When it comes to language and expressing their ideas, these two individuals are the most nitpicky and particular of all the signs. They both value precision in speech and have a tendency to search for the very best way to say or do something, rejecting "lesser" ideas or plans for seemingly small reasons, sometimes to a neurotic degree. The irony is, each can find this mutual perfectionism highly irritating in the other, as they mirror a quality within themselves that is difficult to see objectively. They can get into battles trying to get the other to adopt their point of view. If not handled with compassionate awareness, this can become an unhealthy pattern. They have to be careful not to force their issues on each other. Both should direct their hypercritical tendencies where they are useful, like deciphering a legal document or editing a paper. If they can direct these critical energies usefully, and away from each other, their shared clarity of mind, precision of speech, and high standards can engender deep mutual respect and build the foundation for a fruitful and harmonious relationship.

Mercury Gemini / Mercury Libra

♊   ♎

When two air signs like Mercury Gemini and Mercury Libra come together, they usually bask in the enjoyment they share in each other's conversation. Intellectual discussion is food for both their souls. The realm of the mind is where they are both happiest. Mercury Libra will be dazzled by Mercury Gemini's adaptable brain, lively way with words, and overtly curious nature. Mercury Gemini will be captivated by Mercury Libra's elegance and logical approach to life. In social situations, Mercury Libra, who possesses considerable social finesse, will smooth any ruffled feathers caused by Mercury Gemini—who, easily bored, is quick to let others know when he or she is ready to move on. Other elemental placements (fire, earth, and water) might find this pairing somewhat exhausting, as Mercury Gemini and Mercury Libra have a tendency to talk a lot. Others may feel like outsiders to their conversations and have trouble keeping up with all the concepts and ideas they bandy about. Both Mercury Libra and Mercury Gemini are skilled at seeing the multiple facets of any issue, which makes them empathetic to each other and likely to be in agreement over big decisions. Between the two of them, Mercury Libra is more likely to have difficulty making up his or her mind. Mercury Libras are inclined to carefully weigh every decision or judgement and can get caught in an intellectual limbo as a result, where seeing merit to many positions hampers their ability to take action. Mercury Gemini expresses his or her ability to "see both sides" through a preference for dabbling and exploring, trying out many activities or even opinions in order to determine what feels right to them. In this way, they balance each other nicely: when Mercury Gemini skims too lightly through life, Mercury Libra will bring the focus back to the here and now. When Mercury Libra vacillates too much as they weigh opposing points of view, Mercury Gemini will remind them to make a decision so they can move on to whatever comes next. These two soar when they are together because of their shared love of anything that expands the mind.

♊ ♏

The mingling of these two energies is like an interesting combination of foods that, while worth experiencing, you're not sure you'd want for a steady diet. Here we have the intense Mercury Scorpio, whose favorite way of communicating is nonverbal. Mercury Gemini, of course, is the master of verbal artistry, but they don't like to dig too deep. The two have fundamentally different approaches to connecting with other people. When each must confront the other's style, this can lead to a shift in perspective that is temporarily energizing, much like that unusual food. Mercury Gemini may find Mercury Scorpio's passion stimulating, and Mercury Scorpio will resonate with Mercury Gemini's inquiring mind. But the energy it takes for them to sustain this relationship, with Mercury Gemini struggling to feel heard and Mercury Scorpio struggling to feel seen, can be draining. When these two get entangled in a disagreement, there can be a lot of frustration. They have a tendency to dig in their heels and stay on opposite sides of a situation, waiting for the other to commit to their logic. Mercury Scorpio rarely submits to anything, however. At first, Mercury Gemini might enjoy trying to win over Mercury Scorpio, but their already limited patience may cause them to simply walk away. The fundamental differences between the ways their minds operate and how they communicate will require sustained commitment to a shared end goal for them to overcome their dissimilarity—but it will be well worth it.

Mercury Gemini / Mercury Sagittarius

♊ ♐

These two are on opposite sides of the zodiac wheel, and as is the case with many opposites, they complement and balance each other unusually well, each bringing to the other something the other lacks. Mercury Gemini believes that problems can be solved by using the intellect. Mercury Sagittarius, who has a mind that is like an open channel, is happy to bring forth the subjects and topics for Mercury Gemini to thoroughly enjoy figuring out. Both are fond of doing several things at once. Both love to talk and meet people. Together they will jump from one topic to another. Mercury Sagittarius will not remember the details, whereas Mercury Gemini will remember everything. There is a synergy to their communication: whether working on a project together, discussing how to solve problems, or enjoying an intellectual debate, these two trade and volley ideas with ease. The positive, stimulating energy of the back-and-forth tends to generate not only improved intellectual and emotional well-being for both but creative ideas in which the whole is greater than the sum of the parts. The only major requirement for peace in this relationship is for them each to give the other space as needed. Neither likes to be caged in by intense emotional discussions. Both prefer to deal with things as they come up, then move on. Mercury Gemini can be hard to pin down, as their minds are often flitting here, there, and everywhere. Mercury Sagittarius can be equally difficult to contain. The beauty of this combination is their mutual love, and true need, for more and more knowledge. Each loves to open up worlds of wisdom and share what they find with the other.

♊ ♑

Mercury Capricorn enjoys frequent practical discussions about everyday life matters. Mercury Gemini will tolerate such talks, which they basically find mundane, yet they will not enjoy them. The practicalities of everyday life are probably Mercury Gemini's least favorite topic of conversation. Mercury Gemini likes to expand. Mercury Capricorn prefers to contract. Mercury Gemini is a big-picture thinker who enjoys the bird's-eye view. Mercury Capricorn prefers to keep their head down and focus on what is in front of them. To Mercury Gemini, Mercury Capricorn can seem rigid or concerned with the banal. To Mercury Capricorn, Mercury Gemini can seem flighty and ungrounded. And that's before they even begin really trying to understand each other. Their verbal styles make connecting even more difficult. Mercury Capricorn does not express themselves easily. Before they speak, they pass every thought through a test inside their mind before sharing anything. This test determines the worth, practicality, and functionality of whatever it is they're going to say. Mercury Gemini couldn't care less about Mercury Capricorn's tough verbal filter. Mercury Gemini lets words flow, and they figure things out by talking through them. To Mercury Capricorn, this can seem like a lack of concern. To Mercury Gemini, Mercury Capricorn can seem willfully reserved and stodgy.

Mercury Gemini / Mercury Aquarius

♊ ♒

These two are likely to share such a strong intellectual magnetism that whatever becomes of their relationship down the road, they will never forget the scintillating conversations they shared. In part, this is because both come from the air realm, and there is an easy and natural flow to their streams of logic. This is especially soothing and invigorating to Mercury Aquarius, who, being the verbal free spirit of the zodiac, is used to being misunderstood. A person with Mercury in Aquarius typically has a very eccentric mind. This is the person at the dinner party who will blurt out an opinion that others find outrageous or completely out of the blue, just to alleviate the monotony. Expansive Mercury Gemini, who delights in controversy, gets a kick out of their spontaneous comments. Both have a large number of intellectual interests, and their mutual well-developed sense of curiosity will serve the relationship well. There is a wonderful mental affinity between these two. They inspire each other and find a lot of commonality in their outlooks on life.

♊ ♓

Mercury Pisces dispenses with logical processes and relies on instinct and emotions when making a decision. Mercury Gemini tends to view things in a super-rational way. Mercury Pisces is prone to changing their mind, as they have a habit of weighing their options at length, trying to decide which will lead to the outcome that feels the best. Mercury Gemini will do the same thing, but it is not about what feels best; it is what logically works best. For Mercury Pisces, this more emotional viewpoint is a sensible defensive strategy, but to Mercury Gemini this behavior can seem extremely wishy-washy. On the surface it would seem that Mercury Pisces and Mercury Gemini share this quality of indecisiveness. But where Mercury Pisces is motivated by emotion, the "flightiness" of the far more emotionally contained Mercury Gemini is motivated by curiosity and the risk of boredom. This comes out in how each expresses themselves verbally, as well. Mercury Gemini has a far more logical mind and tongue than Mercury Pisces, who—given their ultrasensitivity—could find this annoying. Both also have a duality to their natures. The symbol of Gemini is the twins, and for Pisces it is two fish. But instead of bringing them closer or helping them to understand each other, this seemingly shared quality can cause frustration. Their tendencies toward duality can keep them circling in discussions for a while, leading to a hopeless feeling that they aren't making progress in a particular direction. While there is some possibility for connection here based on their kindred artistic aptitudes, overall there is a tendency for this to be a problematic pairing.

MERCURY CANCER

A PERSON WITH MERCURY IN CANCER IS GOING TO BE more sensitive to tone of voice and choice of words than most of the other Mercury signs in the zodiac. If someone raises their voice or speaks harshly, Mercury Cancer will leave the room. They patently detest arguing. There is not an ounce of their being that enjoys any kind of verbal intensity. If you need someone to comfort you with soft words when you are upset, you can count on Mercury Cancer. They would never tell you to "buckle down and get over it!" This Mercury placement understands that emotions are supposed to be felt, and if you need to sit with your feelings for some time, they are totally supportive. Living in the realm of watery introspection, Mercury Cancer tends to brood over the emotional well-being of themselves and their loved ones. Their minds focus on the things that feed their soul, like food, spirituality, and friendship. The things they care about go deep into their hearts. The intensity of their feeling can be off-putting to Mercury placements that are more airy or fiery. Being so sensitive to emotions, they may cry if you speak to them in the wrong way. They usually are too sensitive for sarcasm. In their minds, words should to be used to nurture. Because they seem like natural psychologists, people instinctively feel like they can share secrets with Mercury Cancer without fear of being ridiculed. If there is a gentle way to deliver an uncomfortable truth, they will be the ones to figure out the right words. Being highly intuitive, their minds pick up every nuance in a situation or conversation—and other signs' inability to "read" a person as well as they can often frustrates them. Given their retentive minds, it is quite probable that Mercury Cancer will often remember every last detail of their childhood, including the names of grade school teachers and even their locker combinations. Everything related to childhood means a lot to Mercury Cancer. They long for the days of youthful innocence and sometimes have a tendency to be wistful about the past.

MERCURY CANCER COMBINATIONS

Mercury Cancer / Mercury Cancer

♋ ♋

This is a tremendously supportive combination. They share a cosmic rapport where all of their emotions are easily accepted and understood. Each has a huge desire to express what they are feeling, especially to someone who can listen with gentleness and who will not try to change their thinking. They are likely to meet about food, money, and matters having to do with the home. The symbol of Cancer is the crab—and these two are like hermit crabs, carrying their home, or the concept of home, wherever they go. When they come together, they enjoy sharing discussions about their lives inside their protective shells. The bond is so powerful that when they're together it might feel as if the rest of the world is shut out. It is very difficult for either of them to hide anything from the other, since they seem to telepathically read each other's unconscious thoughts. Sometimes it can feel as if they have so many shared emotional experiences that they have melted into one being. There is a lot of instinctive alchemy going on here. The danger lies in both becoming despondent through an excess of sympathetic emotions. Watching the evening news can be painful for this pair, as they will watch and retain whatever trauma is going on, almost feeling too much sympathy for those less fortunate.

Mercury Cancer / Mercury Leo

♋ ♌

Here we have the Cancer crab, with its hard exterior shell protecting its soft, sensitive inside, meeting the powerful and muscular lion, Leo. Mercury Leo relates to everything in a larger-than-life fashion. When Mercury Leo wants to roar, they roar, in words that are powerful and booming. To Mercury Cancer this can feel like a verbal assault, and they will duck and hide when the lion is going full tilt. And yet, they oddly understand each other, as each possesses a quality the other longs for: Mercury Cancer sometimes wishes for the verbal stage presence that Mercury Leo comes by naturally. And Mercury Leo sees—and envies—how many friends Mercury Cancer has because of their gentle approach with people. That said, Mercury Leo is the verbal cheerleader of the zodiac. They are naturally optimistic and positive thinkers, whereas Mercury Cancer tends to be the consummate worrywart. Mercury Cancer can enjoy the glowing positivity of Mercury Leo, as long as Mercury Leo remembers to be a sweet little pussycat once in a while. Sometimes a meow will suffice.

Mercury Cancer / Mercury Virgo

♋ ♍

When Mercury Virgo meets Mercury Cancer, either the interaction can be pleasant, in a simple, straightforward way, or it can feel like being stuck in mud. When the water of Cancer meets the earth of Virgo, there is a nice blending of energies, as both can get obsessed with details. But the kinds of detail the two care about are quite different: Mercury Cancer fixates on the emotional aspects of life, while Mercury Virgo's obsession is with the practical details of daily life—crossing every "i" and dotting every "t." They can both be myopic, but especially Mercury Virgo— because they both crave stability and seek situations and environments that are free of drama. This can be a great pair as siblings, as colleagues, and as friends, but they have to work at thriving as a couple. Though they will enjoy each other's homey nature and down-to-earth qualities, neither will overly challenge the other to grow or change. Pretty soon, that comfort can turn to complacency, which can turn to boredom. Both of them need to guard against too much introspection, leading to calcification of the brain. Breaking patterns and changing routines will keep these two in a good place.

♋ ♎

The symbol of Libra is the scales, which judge and determine what is balanced and fair. When a person's Mercury is in Libra, they will be particularly consumed by trying to determine the fairest outcome. But because they are skilled at seeing a multiplicity of perspectives, they may take much longer than other Mercury signs to weigh their options about how to act or what to say. They may even second-guess themselves, suddenly seeing an angle they hadn't considered before, and vacillate between choices. Mercury Cancer is not overly invested in having intellectual discussions and weighing options. All they want to do is shake the Mercury Libra person and say, "Just go with your heart and your gut! What is your intuition telling you?" Well, Mercury Libra does not operate from this world of emotional feelings. They are more about logic and appreciating what makes sense from a rational point of view. Though this seeming lack of emotion can frustrate Mercury Cancer, at the same time, Mercury Libra's essential diplomacy is a balm to the sensitive Mercury Cancer. When Mercury Libra is operating at the highest level possible, they are the masters of finding and saying just the right word, a quality that Mercury Cancer dearly requires in any sustainable relationship. Though they can get bogged down by their equally weighty but markedly different communication styles—one being so rooted in reason and the other in emotion—air and water signs have the potential for joyful lightness. Think of a glass of champagne: when air (Libra) meets liquid (Cancer), bubbles happen.

♋ ♏

This can be a mentally intoxicating combination. Water meets water, and like a river that flows to the sea, these two easily combine and delve into the realm of deep intimate thoughts. Mercury Scorpio's mind is probing, passionate, and intensely private. Mercury Cancer is drawn to Mercury Scorpio's quest for answers regarding the mysteries of life. Both are sensitive to the nuances of words. Neither enjoys people who use a sharp tone of voice. Of the two, Mercury Scorpio is the one more likely to verbally dish it out, if confronted. It takes an extreme situation to get Mercury Cancer to raise their voice. Mercury Scorpio is far more secretive and suspicious than Mercury Cancer. Mercury Scorpio enjoys discovering people's subconscious desires. Mercury Cancer is happy to let Mercury Scorpio do all the digging and then report back with their findings. There is a blending here of intuition and instincts. Both can be dedicated to an ideal, which they will both willingly fight for. Introspection is their mutual feeding ground, and they are happiest knowing the other is there keeping them company.

Mercury Cancer / Mercury Sagittarius

♋ ♐

This is a tough combination. Mercury Cancer enjoys the playfulness of Mercury Sagittarius but can do without the teasing that oftentimes comes with it. They're also not fond of Mercury Sagittarius's sarcasm, which is a hallmark of their speaking style. Mercury Sagittarius enjoys philosophical discussions, and though Mercury Cancer is a reflective sign and they tend to be deep thinkers, they are at odds even in this seeming similarity: Mercury Sagittarius likes exploring big, lofty subjects like history, religion, literature, while Mercury Cancer focuses on more personal and intimate concerns. Mercury Sagittarius can also be snobbish and judgmental. They believe everyone should be developing their intellects—but only through the pursuits Mercury Sagittarius deems worthwhile or interesting. When others do something in a non–Mercury Sagittarius approved way or express an idea that contradicts Mercury Sagittarius's way of thinking, they are likely to dismiss them outright, saying something like, "That idea is so stupid and if you don't agree with me then you're just an idiot." They don't really care if they offend. It is not that they mean to be tough, but sometimes they just don't stop to notice that they have blurted out something that really wasn't sensitive. From their point of view, they have wisdom and professional opinions that should not be ignored. With Mercury Cancer deeply disliking anyone who uses words in a less-than-sensitive fashion, they would need very thick skin to handle the Mercury Sagittarius tongue.

♋ ♑

Though Mercury Cancer can have a quirky sense of humor, in general there is not a lot of lightness of spirit to the way their mind works—but compared to Mercury Capricorn they are practically comedians. Playful banter does not come easily to Mercury Capricorns (mind you, this doesn't mean they are humorless, just that their sense of humor is not always immediately evident). There is a seriousness to their mind, voice, and choice of words. They are all about concision: Mercury Capricorn believes in using the fewest words possible to get a point across. They are the pragmatists of the zodiac. If you do not stress the utilitarian value of something, they will not be interested. Though they choose their words with care, hating waste, Mercury Capricorn is still likely to aggravate the more emotional and sensitive Mercury Cancer, who may find them too clinical and unfeeling. As for Mercury Capricorn, they are likely to find Mercury Cancer moody and overly driven by feelings. That said, this pair can get along well, especially in a professional setting, because Mercury Capricorn likes to feel as if they are the boss, and Mercury Cancer, who craves stability, will enjoy the way Mercury Capricorn takes over as leader. It is as if Mercury Capricorn brings structure to the emotional whirlwinds that swirl inside Mercury Cancer's head on a daily basis, bringing a feeling of coming home to a safe harbor.

Mercury Cancer / Mercury Aquarius

♋ ♒

In this combination, a bohemian, big-picture thinker (Mercury Aquarius) meets an emotional, self-focused thinker (Mercury Cancer) with mixed results. The pairing can work, but it might never feel entirely "right." Mercury Aquarius loves the world and cares deeply about thinking of ways to improve the future of humanity. Mercury Cancer is more focused on themselves and the here and now, more consumed with quotidian thoughts like "I wonder what I could have for dinner?" Mercury Aquarius, on the other hand, will sometimes forget to eat. A Mercury Aquarius is not usually focused on whatever is front and center. They are always looking forward and out. Though both are basically gentle with their choice of words and have a tendency toward kindness, however, their viewpoints are so vastly different that they have a hard time understanding each other's values. The Mercury Cancer mind is touchy-feely; they take things personally, whereas the Mercury Aquarius mind is more detached by nature. They are likely to be so busy exploring all the possibilities of this big wide world that they forget Mercury Cancer asked them to do some simple task. To Mercury Cancer, this could feel like an indication that Mercury Aquarius doesn't care about them. This is a bit of a challenging interplay. It is could feel just plain quirky at best.

Mercury Cancer / Mercury Pisces

♋ ♓

At times, these two may feel as if they are reading each other's minds telepathically. Both water signs, they share an easy flow of communication, their thoughts and ideas mixing together so well that they might appear to be almost indistinguishable. Sometimes they hardly have to rely on words at all. This bond is satisfying to both parties. There is a high level of emotional compatibility, as they indulge in emotional discussions regarding their every little feeling. Indulging *too* frequently or at too great length in sharing emotional truths is the only downside to this pairing. Both would be better served at times by extricating themselves from their intense focus on their feelings, getting out of their heads and into the world. Staying grounded is crucial to both Mercury Cancer and Mercury Pisces, as both possess high levels of psychic sensitivity and are unusually attuned to the unseen world. Mercury Pisces in particular learns through a sensing/feeling process, as opposed to straight logic, and of the two, they are far less pragmatic than Mercury Cancer. However deep they go in their communing, it will almost always be Mercury Cancer who breaks the spell and says, "That was fun, but can we go out to dinner now?" Though this is crucial and necessary to their well-being, it may irritate Mercury Pisces. But if they can both handle that small difference in a satisfactory manner, then this is a happy and easy combination.

MERCURY LEO

THE MERCURY LEO MIND OPERATES AT HIGH SPEED. They are spontaneous by nature and impatient with people who require complex preplanning. Procrastinators drive them nuts. When they conceive of an idea, they like to act on it, now! Just as a lion (their symbol) has a powerful roar, people with Mercury Leo have a strong voice that they are not afraid to use, especially when defending their loved ones. "Meek" is not a word most people would use to describe the speaking style of a Mercury Leo. Some might call them passionate, others, well . . . loud. It's not uncommon for a Mercury Leo to have a big, booming voice. They are articulate and often dramatic. Where another Mercury placement might compliment someone by saying,

"What a nice dress you are wearing," Mercury Leo would say, "That dress is so adorable! You look fantastic!" Most people would be content with saying that the dress is nice, but with Mercury Leo everything is absolute and usually more expansive. There is a larger-than-life quality to their words. Their opinions tend to sound like pronouncements, so they have to guard against coming across as grandiose or boastful. They also have a tendency to feel their opinions are the only correct ones and to perceive those who disagree with them as disloyal. Mercury Leo doesn't intend to be so dramatic, but their wiring prevents them from doing or saying anything half-heartedly. At the same time, because they speak with a great deal of warmth, others usually find them quite charming and highly persuasive. For this reason, they make excellent motivational speakers. When a Mercury Leo believes in you, likes you, or loves you, you will feel as if you are around your biggest fan. However, when the soft touch is needed, with the tender voice, Mercury Leo has to work hard at toning it down. They are like a shining light that doesn't have a dimmer switch.

MERCURY LEO COMBINATIONS

♌ ♌

Naturally, when fire meets fire, there is a great deal of affinity. There can be a lot of verbal intensity with these two, however. Both feel that they should be the center of attention, and the struggle for dominance in that regard can be problematic if they spend too much time vying for that position. In a productive pairing of two Mercury Leos, they will be able to fluidly trade places, switching off occupying the center stage. They have to be careful of burning each other out, though, as their exchanges tend to be so heightened. That said, this is a direct and friendly combination overall. Both were born to enjoy life. They tend to embark on paths that involve adventure and some risk taking. Neither is verbally conservative, especially when it comes to flattery. One will pay a compliment to the other, and that person will pay an equally gushing compliment in return. And their praise of each other is sincere. When they argue there can be a lot of fierce words, but once the argument passes they will return to their normal state, which is to glow from the warmth of the other's verbal appreciation. The only danger here is if they get into battles with their egos. If they think from their big hearts first, it will help to ensure harmony, and they can remain members of their mutual admiration society.

♌ ♍

Mercury Virgo is eminently reasonable. They like to be useful, and their approach to communication and problem solving is rooted in that desire: they want everything to function as efficiently as possible and at its highest level. They are detail oriented and can be compulsive about making sure everything is in place. Mercury Leo appreciates that Mercury Virgo dots every "i" and crosses every "t" and that their plans are so thoughtful, and will often tell them so. But Mercury Leo, who operates from the heart, prefers to fly by the seat of their pants. When they feel passionately about something, whether positive or negative, you can be sure you will hear about it. They don't always have the patience for Mercury Virgo and their fixation on determining a logical sequence to how things should be done, or their need to process everything through their reasonable mind. If Mercury Leo can exercise patience around Mercury Virgo and appreciate the balance and sanity they bring, then this can be a productive pairing. For Mercury Virgo, focusing on the magnanimous nature, creativity, and warmth and passion of Mercury Leo will keep in check their potential frustration. As long as they don't try to convert the other to their way of thinking, this can be an enjoyable interaction.

♌ ♎

There is something regal about how these two individuals relate to each other. Leo's symbol is the lion king, and a royal aura surrounds any planet that falls into Leo. Libra's symbol is the scale of justice—think of a Supreme Court justice wearing a robe. These two signs are characterized by a sense of quiet power. Mercury Libra, who is essentially diplomatic and tactful, loves that Mercury Leo expresses thoughts with such emotion. Mercury Leo's larger-than-life pronouncements often humor Mercury Libra's more sedate way of expressing themselves. When Mercury Libra is around Mercury Leo, they lighten up considerably. They are a great team when it comes to any kind of project planning: Mercury Leo brings panache while Mercury Libra brings elegance, and neither is content with the humdrum. This is the kind of pairing that would throw the ideal dinner party: Mercury Libra would set the most beautiful table and invite intriguing guests. Mercury Leo would greet everyone at the door with such a big welcome that everyone would feel instantly at home. This pairing can be wonderfully simpatico in multiple contexts, either professionally or personally: Mercury Libra is committed to creating outcomes that are first class and is not interested in anything less, and that suits Mercury Leo just fine. The only possible difficulty with this pair is when Mercury Libra's indecisiveness comes into play. They like to weigh all options and can worry about choosing the optimal one. Mercury Leo wants to make a decision and be done with it. When Mercury Libra begins second-guessing the dinner party menu—"Should we serve filet mignon tonight after all? Or would you rather have sirloin steaks?"—Mercury Leo can lose patience. Mercury Leo doesn't really care. Just make a decision and put it on the grill. Mercury Libra strives for perfection, which is a beautiful thing, but sometimes this can get out of hand. Mercury Leo will help Mercury Libra realize that perfection can be boring. And Mercury Libra will help Mercury Leo tone down their sometimes over-the-top sense of verbal drama.

Mercury Leo / Mercury Scorpio

♌ ♏

These are two very intense Mercury placements. Mercury Leo's mind is fast and confident. Leo is the sign of the king, and to rule their kingdom they sometimes need to make proclamations and do so with great assurance. Mercury Scorpio's mind is shrewd and sharp. They are fascinated by many topics and love to plumb the depths regarding the mysteries of life. When paired, their equally powerful but extremely different minds may clash at the deepest levels. That said, there is also the possibility of a strong connection between the two, because they are likely to recognize their intellectual equal in the other and feel a tacit respect for the other's intensity. They both place a lot of importance on being recognized, but the difference is that Mercury Leo wants to be acknowledged publicly and Mercury Scorpio wants to be known at a deeply personal level. They may unconsciously compete with each other. Mercury Leo wants their thoughts to be heard. Mercury Scorpio also demands to have their opinions acknowledged. But Mercury Leo achieves this by charming people with skillful repartee, whereas Mercury Scorpio does it by looking deep into someone's eyes and asking, "Tell me what moves you." Mercury Leo is like a lion basking in the sunshine on top of a rock. Mercury Scorpio is like a scorpion, lurking behind that rock in the cool shade. As is always the case, fire signs (Leo) are more outward and water signs (Scorpio) are more inward. These two are very different yet equally strong-minded. There is no way that either one will be successful in changing the other person's mind, so the best solution is to agree to disagree with respect. This can be a very powerful combination, but there must be a willingness on both sides to completely accept that everyone is entitled to their own opinion and who is to say what is right?

Mercury Leo / Mercury Sagittarius

♌ ♐

The symbol of Sagittarius is the centaur, a mythical creature that is half human and half horse. At the heart of a Mercury Sagittarius's way of communicating is a struggle between their impulsive animal mind and their intellectual human mind. However, this interplay between the animal mind and the human mind lends them an essentially playful and adventurous nature. They love to play practical jokes and to tease, yet they can have a tendency to take jokes a little too far, using language that can feel hurtful instead of funny. This is compounded by their sharp intellect and quick-wittedness, which can lead them to express their rather pointed thoughts a bit too quickly, before considering how their words might affect others. But if anyone can deal with their spirited way of speaking, it is Mercury Leo. This is because Mercury Leo can anticipate Mercury Sagittarius's brain waves, which move at a fast speed. Both are fire signs, and they both have a knack for being mentally agile. Mercury Leo also shares Mercury Sagittarius's childlike style of play. They want to travel and see the world, and both enjoy romping around museums, sporting events, and any other place that expands their minds. It will most likely be Mercury Sagittarius who will lead the charge for novelty in the relationship. This is because the Mercury Sagittarius mind is one of the most insatiable. Mercury Leo will not get exasperated when Mercury Sagittarius gets irritated by those who are not as clear thinking as they think they are. These two have a lot of life energy to their conversations, and when they meet up it is rarely boring.

Mercury Leo / Mercury Capricorn

♌ ♑

Here we have the introverted Mercury Capricorn meeting the extroverted Mercury Leo—at least when it comes to communication styles. Mercury Capricorn tends to be verbally reticent and reserved, whereas Mercury Leo is highly expressive and outgoing. Mercury Capricorn's symbol is the goat. The goat can climb any mountain, and Mercury Leo will respect the passion that Mercury Capricorn puts into scaling multiple summits. Mercury Leo's symbol is the lion. The lion commands authority, and Mercury Capricorn will admire Mercury Leo's ability to be decisive and take action. Both look up to each other's ambitious natures. But at the end of the day, Mercury Capricorn is too mentally introverted for the more extroverted Mercury Leo. Mercury Capricorn will have a hard time praising Mercury Leo more than a few times a week, and Mercury Leo will be frustrated when Mercury Capricorn can't tell them how wonderful they are at least once a day. This can be a great lesson for Mercury Leo, however, in pulling back from their ego. For Mercury Capricorn, this can be a good opportunity to step outside their comfort zone and practice knowing that some people quite simply need more attention than others.

Mercury Leo / Mercury Aquarius

♌ ♒

The Mercury Aquarius mind focuses on the big picture: they are humanitarians who believe deeply in personal freedom and equality and are interested in the advancement of humankind. Because of this, they tend to be very open-minded about a variety of topics and yet to some they may seem quirky or eccentric. Mercury Leo infuses Mercury Aquarius's expansive mind with nurturing support and a strong belief that anything is possible. Ideas flow easily between the two of them. They both have a knack for idealism, but it is Mercury Leo who will add the touch of pizzazz to the equation. Mercury Aquarius is gifted at speaking difficult truths in a way that people can hear, bringing softness to Mercury Leo's sometimes abrasive style. All the fire sign placements of Mercury have a tendency to offend people with their words. However, it is Mercury Leo who is most likely to realize the power of teaming up with someone with that special gift of being a peacemaker, and that is Mercury Aquarius. This allows Mercury Leo to play the role of the entertainer. The two of them collaborate well, because they each bring to the table something that the other is missing. Together they can develop ingenious concepts to change a small community or an entire nation. When you combine the innovative brain of Mercury Aquarius with Mercury Leo's charm, they can mesmerize almost anyone. Overall this is a lovely combination, especially since there is often a lot of innovation here.

♌ ♓

Mercury Pisces has a dreamy mind. They are happiest drifting in the world of enchantment and imagination. Highly intuitive, they follow their feelings rather than facts and can be hard to pin down. While the expressive side of Mercury Leo enjoys Mercury Pisces's ability to conjure up magic, when it comes to actual resonance in the conversational realm, these two are like night and day. Mercury Leo is like the sun. They broadcast their ideas as if they are rays of light meant to penetrate the darkness. They have a regal attitude—certain and self-assured—about their pronouncements. Mercury Pisces is like the sea. The way they speak resembles the constant rolling of the waves: one thought bleeds into the next, and it can be hard to isolate distinct ideas or clear statements. To a Mercury Leo, listening to a Mercury Pisces can be excruciating, an extreme test of patience. They perceive Mercury Pisces as rambling and unable to get to the point. To Mercury Pisces, Mercury Leo will feel pedantic and bossy. Their self-assurance may come across as arrogance, and their unwillingness to tease out possibilities may feel rigid. So how do these two manage to handle their differences? The trick is to focus on the fact that both are greatly moved by things they care about. There is a heightened sense of what is possible with these two. If they can keep their visions unified, all will be well.

MERCURY VIRGO

VIRGO IS THE MOST PRACTICAL AND ANALYTICAL OF the earth signs. When Mercury is found in Virgo, the individual has a very efficient mind, with a natural ability to distill complex information into bite-sized pieces. A Mercury Virgo can take a multifaceted subject and condense it into its essence. They meet life as if it consists of a series of problems they need to solve. Hungry to find precise meanings, this type enjoys the details. They are the consummate editor, craftsman, fact checker, dentist, or accountant. This is a strong placement, since the planet Mercury is traditionally considered the ruler of Virgo. These are individuals who like to please and make everything nice. They will remember where they put their keys, pay their bills on time, and probably put together that new vacuum cleaner without even looking at the directions. Sometimes they like order so much that they can become nags, especially when other Mercury signs are not as precise as they are. Not big fans of coarse or foul language, these are the folks who will correct improper grammar. Because they have such a strong sense of properness, these individuals have to guard against coming across as too critical; Mercury Virgo can become compulsive about making everything more efficient and better. While not a cruel placement, it certainly is an exacting one. Therefore, to help facilitate harmony with other Mercury types, Mercury Virgo might consider living by the motto "Stop thinking and just let things happen." Being eminently practical has its rewards, however their dedication to orderliness and functionality can become frustrating for others who would love for them to lighten up. A little human silliness is important to keep them happy.

MERCURY VIRGO COMBINATIONS

....
Mercury Virgo / Mercury Virgo
....

♍ ♍

When two logical thinkers merge, they improve everything around them. They will organize the closets, pay the bills on time, and follow complex recipes to a T. They have excellent memories and can retain information in ways that few others can. If paired up in a business or financial project, they are likely to rise together to a prominent position, because they excel at getting things done. Others may find them lacking in spontaneous thoughts; however, it's not that they aren't creative thinkers. Their creative thought is born from a rigorous type of analysis, which is creative in its own right. Their innate reserve and sensitivity keeps them more verbally subdued than most other Mercury placements. In fact, some may misinterpret this reserve as indifference. However, they are not passive people. They just process their thoughts at a different pace. Mercury Virgos feel that a few carefully chosen words can have a much greater impact than many imprecise words. In this pairing, each individual can handle the critical tendencies of the other because both silently understand that making everything better is the primary goal. Overall, this pairing is a meeting of the minds that satisfies both individuals.

Mercury Virgo / Mercury Libra

There is some compatibility in this pairing because both individuals appreciate fairness and balance. However, problems may arise between these two due to their diverging verbal approaches to achieving harmony. Both Mercury Virgo and Mercury Libra have picky minds. However, Mercury Virgo is less calm than Mercury Libra. Mercury Virgo wants to be useful and thrives on using words as perfectly as possible. Therefore, they get upset when others are not equally fastidious about language. Mercury Libra always loves balance and soothing conversation, but they are not as emotionally invested in having every conversation mean something. Mercury Libra can adapt to their differences, but Mercury Virgo will get irritated when Mercury Libra is more detached. There is an element of duty associated with Mercury Virgo's way of thinking. However, Mercury Libra doesn't feel quite as responsible and, therefore, doesn't get as worked up as Mercury Virgo. Eventually, Mercury Libra may get tired of Mercury Virgo's criticisms. Mercury Virgo, on the other hand, may become weary of hearing Mercury Libra talk as if they want the same things but not feeling it is really true.

Mercury Virgo / Mercury Scorpio

♍ ♏

The practicality of the Mercury Virgo mind and the curiosity of the Mercury Scorpio mind create an intriguing combination. Mercury Scorpio is massively curious, which is attractive to Mercury Virgo, who does not naturally dive into deep thinking. Mercury Scorpio can be very deductive to the more puritanical Mercury Virgo, who willingly follows Mercury Scorpio into new intellectual territories. This novel way of thinking catches Mercury Virgo off guard in a good way. While normally rather regimented in their thinking, Mercury Virgo lets their proverbial hair down when hooked up with Mercury Scorpio. Things do not have to be as "perfect" as was first desired. Mercury Scorpio's mind can penetrate Mercury Virgo's rigidity so well that others may be surprised when Mercury Virgo really loosens their tight grip under Mercury Scorpio's influence. Mercury Scorpio enjoys the practical benefits of Mercury Virgo's more utilitarian way of thinking. Together they can excel in joint projects, as each has a deep capacity for loyalty when it comes to shared goals.

Mercury Virgo / Mercury Sagittarius

Mercury Virgo and Mercury Sagittarius cannot go long before disagreeing about something. Both signs are very demanding, but in different ways. Mercury Sagittarius likes people's ideas to be forthright and prefers a pointed, bull's-eye approach to problem solving. Mercury Virgo—the quintessential problem solver—can be equally demanding. However, Mercury Virgo has a logical, precise way of doing things and will get touchy if someone tries to speed up their naturally slow pace or make conflicting demands. When Mercury Sagittarius says, "Hurry up and get on with it!" Mercury Virgo might reply, "When I am good and ready and not a moment before." In addition to conflicting problem-solving styles, these two Mercury signs are likely to have differing opinions on a variety of topics. Mercury Virgo is also far more contained with their speech than Mercury Sagittarius, whose communication style is far freer and more direct. Mercury Sagittarius may find Mercury Virgo to be neurotic, and Mercury Virgo may find Mercury Sagittarius to be pushy. Not exactly a highly compatible connection, but there are always exceptions based on other connections in the charts.

Mercury Virgo / Mercury Capricorn

♍ ♑

Both Mercury Virgo and Mercury Capricorn have minds focused on achieving, and therefore, they enjoy each other's serious work ethics. As they are drawn to one another's sense of order and neatness, there is an air of propriety when these two are together. Of the two signs, Mercury Virgo is more critical than Mercury Capricorn. But Mercury Capricorn can match them with their own exacting style of communication. While Mercury Capricorn is more focused on the final outcome, Mercury Virgo is very much in the present, thinking in a sequential manner about how to get to the finish line. Both signs are obsessed with being punctual and loyal, whether it relates to a goal, a person, or an ideal. No one could run an efficient business or family better than these two. Both signs may need to guard against being a little too serious. Mercury Virgo can get lost in minutiae. Mercury Capricorn can be so stodgy in their thinking that this prevents them from making progress. However, they are compatible thinkers in that they have a similar ability to focus on useful information to get them where they need to go. Time out for fun is what the doctor would order for these two!

Mercury Virgo is the consummate pragmatist; Mercury Aquarius is such a dreamer. How can these two find common ground? Quite simply, they have a choice. Either Mercury Virgo will enjoy the lofty ideas of Mercury Aquarius and help them implement their dreams, or they will become supremely irritated when Mercury Aquarius's thoughts spin off in a million directions. Mercury Aquarius wants to believe that anything is possible, while Mercury Virgo needs proof that something is practical. Mercury Aquarius can either admire Mercury Virgo and their incredible take-charge—and very conventional—approach to making things happen, or they will get worn down by constant comments like "Are you sure this will work?" or "It sounds like a great idea, but how practical is it really?" Talk about having the Virgo needle burst your air bubble! Mercury Virgo doesn't mean to squash dreams, but they are highly protective people and worry that not being practical could have harmful side effects. Mercury Aquarius would never have a dreamy vision if all they thought about were the nitty-gritty practical details. These two just need to live and let live and ultimately revel in their differences. You can't achieve a vision without a plan, and these two actually need each other's brains to balance themselves out.

♍ ♓

Mercury Pisces has finely honed intuition. They are enormously sensitive and can morph their brain to meld with that of another. This fluid mode of thinking is in stark contrast to the precise and organized way that Mercury Virgo processes thoughts. Mercury Pisces has a mind like the ocean—always moving, somewhat disorderly, and often unpredictably so. Mercury Virgo will want to contain Mercury Pisces when they go off on a tangent that doesn't have an obvious point. This drives Mercury Virgo crazy. But Mercury Pisces has a beautiful way of getting Mercury Virgo to put aside their analytical way of thinking for a moment and experience what it feels like to be mystically open. This pairing can be a harmonious combination or a frustrating one. If Mercury Virgo can let go and trust, Mercury Pisces can be a wonderful tour guide into the realms of fantasy and imagination. And if Mercury Pisces allows Mercury Virgo to help their ideas become more concrete and precise, it can be a lovely experience for both parties.

MERCURY LIBRA

MERCURY LIBRA PEOPLE ARE THE MOST LOGICAL thinkers of the zodiac. Their symbol, the scales of justice, represents their constant search for balance and partnerships. Their minds are preoccupied with fairness, so people with this placement make excellent lawyers, judges, or mediators. Libra is an air sign, so there is a detached, cool-headed quality to this Mercury placement. "Civil" is the word I would use to describe their feeling tone and their method of interacting with others. They place value on diplomacy and calm, well-reasoned logic. Desiring peaceful outcomes, they prefer to interact with others who share this same passion for equilibrium. Libra is the only sign of the zodiac that is neither an animal nor a human but instead an inanimate object. On top of that, a scale is intended to weigh and measure; it is inherently cool and clinical. Animals and humans have hearts, but a scale does not. Therefore, the only negative quality of this placement is that they can be too analytical, sometimes aloof, and somewhat cold. There is a danger here of rendering too many judgments, as if in a court of law. Other Mercury placements may find them critical and sometimes arrogant, as if they knew it all. Mercury Libra often needs to learn how to appreciate others' viewpoints and feelings without rendering judgment. A mind that prioritizes fairness and balance is a wonderful thing, of course, but when those qualities are elevated above all else, there is little room left for visceral feeling. There is a lot of potential to please many people with their graceful ability to charm others with words. This talent is both intriguing and beguiling as Mercury Libra skillfully avoids strife.

MERCURY LIBRA COMBINATIONS

Mercury Libra / Mercury Libra

♎ ♎

These two peas in a pod will be the most sought-after dinner guests for any party. They are charming people. Both enjoy learning about others and can talk about a myriad of topics. The art of listening is a rare quality, and both of them have this wonderful talent. Mercury Libra, being obsessed with fairness, is extremely capable of hearing other people's stories and will make others feel as if they are being heard. Because of this quality, people enjoy having them around. When you put two Mercury Libra brains together, they are in total sync. Whatever moves them, whether a piece of music or a novel, they will enjoy discussing all the ingredients that made that particular work of art so outstanding. They love to decide what the best is, and sharing their opinions with each other is fun for them. Fortunately these two will pretty much agree on everything! To outsiders, it may appear that they are mirroring each other's thoughts. This is a combination of two synergistic minds that enjoy weighing the pros and cons of just about everything.

♎ ♏

Mercury Libra likes life to move along in a predictable way. Mercury Scorpio could care less about predictability. All they care about is depth. Mercury Scorpio wonders, "Are our conversations going to reach the inner recesses of our souls?" But Mercury Libra does not thrive in this territory of seething emotional intensity the way Mercury Scorpio does. It is possible that Mercury Libra will bring some fresh perspectives to Mercury Scorpio's constant plunging into emotional topics. But overall there are some great differences in their intellectual and communication styles. Mercury Scorpio demands attention while Mercury Libra likes to keep everything balanced and emotionally neutral. Mercury Scorpio doesn't know the meaning of neutral, however. With them, everything is either a high or a low. The middle is hard for them to reach. Mercury Libra loves the middle. Perhaps there will be moments of peace, as they both can appreciate their different viewpoints, but there is an inherent difficulty here.

There is a lovely comingling of energies here, as the air of Mercury Libra ignites the fire of Mercury Sagittarius. Both of them know how to dazzle in the social world. Mercury Libra is charming and could easily be called the consummate diplomat. Mercury Sagittarius is the quick-witted raconteur, who delights a crowd with rapid-fire jokes or playful puns. They share a strong understanding of each other's mental abilities, without ever feeling competitive or cramped by the other person's style. That said, Mercury Libra has a more refined communication style, whereas Mercury Sagittarius can be coarse. Mercury Libra will always try to say just the right thing, while Mercury Sagittarius is just plain blunt. They may find their different approaches a curious thing, and they quite often will marvel at the other without getting upset.

Mercury Libra / Mercury Capricorn

♎ ♑

Even though there is an undeniable attraction between these two, the pairing, both platonically and romantically, can be quite tense. Mercury Capricorn, like Mercury Libra, has a mental coolness that can manifest as detachment. Both will sense that detachment and read it as distance. As a result, in a sort of self-fulfilling prophecy, both will always keep a certain amount of distance from each other. This is especially difficult for Mercury Capricorn, as the Mercury Capricorn mind is always working overtime. They have a constant desire to do better and know more. It is possible that the two of them can get along, but without a lot of psychological intimacy (which might actually be just fine for some individuals and perfect for certain situations, like work), they could get bored with each other. Both have a desire to get ahead, and in that sense they are alike. Mercury Libra can be very conciliatory and will compromise if need be. Mercury Capricorn can be shrewd and knows how to strategize. In this way they balance each other, and they can suit each other in a strange way.

Mercury Libra / Mercury Aquarius

♎ ♒

These two will be decidedly intrigued by the other. They will love to talk about similar things, like political causes and ways to make the world a better place. Each has a large capacity to hold space for the other's intellectual musings. Friendship is an attractive component of any relationship, and these two would certainly have an easygoing way of relating to each other. Both have great appreciation for the best parts of what it means to be a good human being. Mercury Aquarius is obsessed with humanitarian causes. Their brains are in overdrive in the department of service. Mercury Libra, who is very adept at dialogue and making their point, can be a big asset to Mercury Aquarius's campaigns. When you put these two together, it is as if they both enjoy following the same road map. There is a freshness to this combination, which both will enjoy.

Mercury Libra / Mercury Pisces

♎ ♓

The biggest problem between these two is that they both like to weigh all possibilities. Mercury Libra likes to measure all the different options in their intellectual brain. Mercury Pisces is emotionally going over all possible pathways, and oftentimes has trouble just pulling the trigger. In doing so, they risk getting stuck in the middle and not being able to decide whether to turn left or right. They also both tend to live in their own little world of the way they think things should be. But having dreamy ideals is what brings them to a common ground. They will be quite tolerant of each other's insights, and Mercury Libra will bring calm and peace to the more emotional Mercury Pisces. Sometimes Mercury Pisces will find Mercury Libra to be too logical. And Mercury Libra will get frustrated when all Mercury Pisces wants to do is let their wild imagination gallop along. Again, as with many combinations, all it takes is a basic appreciation of the other and all is well. The question is "Who will make decisions in this relationship?" If not careful, they could remain in limbo, and movement forward could become tough.

MERCURY SCORPIO

PEOPLE WHO HAVE A MERCURY PLACEMENT IN SCOR-
pio are patently unsatisfied with anything but deep introspection. They have a need to uncover the truth behind
everything. This can express itself as a suspicious mind, as
they are constantly searching for what they believe is hidden. A water sign, Mercury Scorpio likes to bathe in the
realms of intrigue. Their minds are drawn to people and
situations that emanate a mischievous, even slightly wicked
energy. Those with Mercury in Scorpio are likely to possess a superdry wit and the type of biting humor that can
throw others off balance. Their sense of humor and their
wordplay will either shock you into silence or knock you
from your chair as you laugh uncontrollably. There is no

middle ground with this placement. Intensity is their key word. Piercing, probing, and determined, they choose words that are often imbued with deeply spiritual or restorative qualities. The opposite can also be true, however: if they are not acting from the highest version of this placement. Their snappy and often cutting retorts can verge on cruel. The suspicious Mercury Scorpio mind also affects their relationships; they can be very suspicious and guarded and wonder often about who has their back. The best thing for Mercury Scorpio is to center their powerful mind by doing some daily meditation practice. Being deeply introspective, they thrive when they take the time to pay attention to their intuitive knowledge. There is a deep and soulful creativity with this placement. Mercury Scorpio, probably more than any other sign, is plugged into the higher realms. Left to simply think in peace or in focused meditation, they can enter a trancelike state, which is where their powerful brains receive all the intuitive hits they need to soar above the mundane.

MERCURY SCORPIO COMBINATIONS

♏ ♏

Water meets water, and the blending of these two Mercury placements can be profoundly comforting because they understand each other's intensity. When you put two deep-thinking and constantly probing minds together, you have the recipe for an intellectual pairing that is extremely passionate. Mercury Scorpio is obsessed with what is "hidden." They thrive when discussing "taboo" topics or philosophical subjects like sex, the occult, the mysteries of life, and psychological issues. Two Mercury Scorpios will find that they are with that rare person who is willing to go as deep as they are. Both have a great deal of intuitive wisdom, and it may seem to outsiders that they are practically telepathic when it comes to communicating with each other. Neither likes to intellectualize or explain everything down to the last detail. For a Mercury Scorpio, the ultimate goal is penetrating to the realms of inner knowingness. They would rather delve than stay at the surface of any topic. Whatever lifts their spirits, like fine music, lovemaking, or a gorgeous piece of writing that moves them will make their hearts happy. At the end of the day, they want to be transformed by something that captures their imagination, always seeking the next encounter with that person, book, or art experience that will adequately alter their life experience and cause some sort of inner transformation. Their minds search for complex ideas that they can mull over, and they strive to find topics that will sustain their curiosity. Mercury Scorpio will always press forward, yearning to understand the meaning of life.

Mercury Scorpio / Mercury Sagittarius

When water (Scorpio) meets fire (Sagittarius), there is often a lot of steam. This can mean some feisty conversations—think of the expression "to let off some steam" when you get into a heated argument. This combination can be either an intellectual haven for both parties, in which they find pleasure and comfort in meeting an equally intense brain, or it can be an absolute battlefield. Both find joy and even adventure setting off on a deep, probing conversation and seeing where it leads. The problem is that Mercury Scorpio likes to dive deep into one subject and stay there. While Mercury Sagittarius loves to go deep as well, they do not want to stay there for too long—they want to be free to mentally roam. They will bristle against Mercury Scorpio's focus and struggle to break free. Mercury Scorpio will try to draw them back, but Mercury Sagittarius dislikes anyone trying to curtail their freedom of movement. There is an exotic element to this pairing, because they are from such different realms. They are so different that the interaction can be vastly entertaining for each for a period of time—and sometimes, a very long time. However, there are so many intrinsic differences in this pair that navigating a smooth path will require patience on both their parts.

For example, if a father has Mercury in Sagittarius, and his daughter has Mercury in Scorpio, the father might want to push his daughter into something that she hasn't had sufficient time to process on her own. He could be short-tempered with her need to sit in her room and ponder a decision for hours, when he quickly figured out what he thinks is best for her. She has a very different mental processing timetable than her lightning-fast father. Ironically, neither is particularly patient, so for this combination to run smoothly, both need to be superconscious about their inherent differences.

Mercury Scorpio / Mercury Capricorn

♏ ♑

These two Mercury placements, though highly dissimilar, counterbalance each other unusually well. Mercury Scorpio is an intuitive visionary thinker, while Mercury Capricorn is practical and business minded. Their differences, when brought together, can lead to a harmonious and productive creative relationship. Mercury Capricorn loves structure. Because of this, they excel at functioning as a sort of container for Mercury Scorpio's probing ideas and deep feeling, giving shape or form to Mercury Scorpio's bigger, hard-to-contain ideas. Mentally, they are both tough as nails and persistent in getting where they want to go. Mercury Scorpio can be a bit of an extremist in this regard, though. They don't really understand the concept of no, and they always believe there is another way to transform any situation. Mercury Capricorn will come along and, in a gentle way, bring practicality to Mercury Scorpio's intensity, actually making the desired outcome more likely since it is grounded in reality. This is a useful partnership for both individuals. Mercury Capricorn will not rest until they achieve what their minds have conceived, and Mercury Scorpio is equally ambitious. Together, with Mercury Scorpio's mental toughness and Mercury Capricorn's quest for the best, they can reach the pinnacle of whatever it is they envision together. These are two intense powerhouses that work well together, actually functioning at a higher level together, because of what the other brings to the partnership, than they do alone.

A person with a Mercury placement in any air sign, like Aquarius, tends to excel at making quick connections with others, as they can carry on a charming conversation and possess an easygoing appeal. Mercury Aquarius will initiate conversations with strangers, from a cab driver to a person waiting in line with them, simply because they enjoy talking with all types of people—and inevitably, those strangers will welcome it. Mercury Scorpio is just the opposite. They are guarded and do not enjoy superficial chattiness in general, as they prefer more serious conversations about "deeper" subjects. Once they do establish a meaningful connection with a person, however, they will talk their ear off about their innermost thoughts and feelings. For Mercury Aquarius, this kind of sharing from Mercury Scorpio may not feel like enjoyable emotional intimacy. Instead, they may feel as if Mercury Scorpio is treating them as a receptacle for their emotional dumping rather than as a conversational partner. Mercury Aquarius finds this irritating because they prefer to keep things less intense. Mercury Scorpio's tendency to have strident opinions will only further frustrate Mercury Aquarius, whose motto is "Live and let live." Meanwhile, Mercury Scorpio may interpret Mercury Aquarius's attention to others and chattiness as a sign that they do not care enough about the depths of Mercury Scorpio's thoughts. It is as if Mercury Aquarius would like to keep things light and open and Mercury Scorpio wants conversations to be compacted into emotionally charged discussions. When dealing with such differences, the key is to use humor. Neither style is right or wrong, just different.

♏ ♓

Two powerhouses of sensitivity meet in this dynamic duo. Here we have water meeting water, and whenever two water elements combine, there is an intrinsic flow. There are no boundaries. Everything merges together. Water is about emotions and sensitivity. These two Mercury signs are usually quite telepathic because they have equally high levels of intuition. When they speak with each other, it is as if the molecules that form their thoughts flow into each other, and the two people become one, as if some intellectual magical alchemy has occurred. Mercury Pisces is a gentle placement; they use words with care. These are not the type of individuals who like to get into verbal arguments. Mercury Scorpio wants to be gentle, but they have a definite edge. If they get upset, they will let you have it. When they are around a fellow water sign, however, they will soften in a way that they are not able to with many of the other Mercury placements. Both of these people live by instincts, and they enjoy being around each other because a lot of times they don't even have to use words. Others might marvel at the way they sometimes communicate through a mutual understanding of nonverbal communication styles, like music and dance.

MERCURY SAGITTARIUS

OF ALL THE MERCURY PLACEMENTS, MERCURY SAG-
ittarius is the most direct when it comes to speaking their
mind. More even than the other fire sign placements, Aries and Leo, Mercury Sagittarius is completely capable of
saying whatever they want and not caring or even noticing that it might offend others. Think of their symbol, the
centaur: the half horse, half man—an archer with bow at
the ready, prepared to let his arrow fly. The sharp, piercing arrow speaks to their ability to utter ideas that can
hit the target with astonishing accuracy but also to their
talent for wounding others with sharp comments. The
arrow is either spot on point or ruthlessly impulsive with
word choices. When they want to make a point, you will

definitely know how they feel. There is no pussyfooting around with these people. If you disagree with them, they might (if not evolved) have no problem telling you that you should reconsider your opinion. When used skillfully, however, the Mercury Sagittarius mind is brilliant. They are intellectually curious and dive into many different subjects, always seeking to expand their minds. They love to travel, and wherever they go, they soak up as much as they can about the history, culture, and customs. They often excel at learning languages. "Voracious" is a key word when it comes to describing the mind of Mercury Sagittarius. Just like fire that consumes the forest, Mercury Sagittarius will devour books (which of course are made from trees). Their libraries are often filled with so many books that they have run out of space to hold their massive collection. They are the most intellectual of the fire signs, and they often have a playful sense of humor. Despite their moodiness—one minute they are optimistic and filled with good humor; the next they are like warriors slicing with their sharp tongues—Mercury Sagittarius's fiery vitality can bring much warmth and light. The trick with this placement is to just remember that fire is fire. When controlled, it is wonderful and life sustaining: it can warm us, cook our food, heat water for a luxurious soak in a bathtub. But it can also burn. Having an awareness of the power is all it takes to keep this verbal fire contained and well informed.

MERCURY SAGITTARIUS COMBINATIONS

When it comes to their interest in philosophy and other high-minded subjects, their love of personal freedom, and their desire to travel the world, these two are perfectly attuned. They see eye-to-eye on most matters but would be wise to remember that they are dealing with a person just as quick-witted and clever as they are. When they disagree, both will dish out heated opinions and strident beliefs intended to dismiss and devalue the other's views. There is a lot of intensity when fire meets fire, and these two know how to fight. They may be having a great time together, laughing and having fun, when one of them lets loose with a quick jab and the other matches it with a counterpunch. Then they might start arguing, because that is what fire likes to do: ignite! Neither of them remembers or holds onto anything that was said in the heat of the moment, and all is forgiven until the next time it happens. They often enjoy the heated exchanges. It is what they were designed to do. Neither likes authority, and both dislike injustice. Well suited to fight for the underdog, these two team up well to crusade for a worthwhile cause. They are both very aspirational and focused on positive thinking.

Mercury Sagittarius / Mercury Capricorn

Mercury Sagittarius might pop into the life of Mercury Capricorn to give them a little rocket boost of fun energy and get them out of their overworked head, which thinks too much. But long term this is a difficult pairing. Mercury Capricorn is a serious and methodical thinker and not particularly enthusiastic in the way they express themselves. To Mercury Sagittarius, it can seem like the Mercury Capricorn feels that they are bearing the weight of the world on their shoulders, and they don't have much patience for that. Mercury Capricorn is not terribly spontaneous. These are practical thinkers who don't make a move unless they have thought things over. This will frustrate Mercury Sagittarius when they want to just take off and have an adventure. Mercury Sagittarius will look at their watch and remind Mercury Capricorn that if they don't get a move on, they will miss out on all the fun. This can work if Mercury Capricorn can humor Mercury Sagittarius once in a while. It won't kill them to go on that roller-coaster ride or take a quick trip to Cuba. It might even be just what they need to get them out of their workaholic mind. For Mercury Sagittarius, Mercury Capricorn's considered way with words is a good lesson to temper their verbal impetuousness.

Mercury Sagittarius / Mercury Aquarius

This is a very positive combination. Both will feel as if the other person gives them the perfect balance of space and quality time. There is no fire without oxygen, so Mercury Sagittarius (fire) especially thrives in a relationship with Mercury Aquarius (air). Mercury Aquarius has a unique and somewhat quirky way of thinking and speaking. Mercury Sagittarius is equally unconventional, though their mode of expressing themselves usually comes with a sharper edge. Both enjoy intellectual debate and big ideas, and their natural playfulness brings lightness to their exchanges. Mercury Aquarius is all about connecting with humanity. Mercury Sagittarius enjoys exploring the world and is open to the extraordinary. Together they will enjoy having great adventures, whether real or in their imaginations. Each will feel joyous about having found the other, as they share their unique insights extremely well.

Mercury Sagittarius / Mercury Pisces

Here we have the mental explorer, Mercury Sagittarius, meeting the mental dreamer, Mercury Pisces. Each could sail away and live in a world of the mind, being perfectly happy until they got home—if they ever got back. Because when we get right down to it, neither of them is very practical. Both dislike routine and anything remotely "boring." How can they function together if neither is particularly skilled or predisposed to dealing with what is in front of them? It can be tricky at best. Neither is focused on things that are stable. Mercury Sagittarius is always looking for the next horizon and is ready to roll on a moment's notice. Mercury Pisces has a mind that wants to focus on the unseen realms. They rely on their deepest yearnings and subconscious thoughts. Both will be able to appreciate the other's point of view, but because neither is particularly grounded, this ends up being a rather detached and impersonal combination. And when Mercury Sagittarius gets upset and lets one of their verbal arrows fly, Mercury Pisces might just swim away.

MERCURY CAPRICORN

MERCURY CAPRICORN INDIVIDUALS ARE EXTREMELY practical, pragmatic thinkers, not known for being dreamers. It's not that they inherently lack the ability or power to be visionary thinkers, however; it's more as if they pass every idea through a filter that asks, "Is this useful?" They have an attunement to the reality of the here-and-now, and they tend to rely more upon tangible thoughts than intuitions. Their brains are wired to be extremely determined and goal oriented. If you need to find someone to get a job done in a timely, organized, and businesslike manner, Mercury Capricorn fits the bill perfectly. Although not particularly verbally assertive, they will speak out when something they strongly believe is endangered. But being so utilitarian can become a problem for Mercury Capricorn. Without carving out some space in which to daydream, they can become so earnestly focused on utility that they become somber and humorless. It will probably take some of the other Mercury placements to get these people out of their thinking ruts. Allowing others to infiltrate their thinking and lighten them up is important to keep them balanced. It will take some time to get their heads out of work mode, but once they make that transition, these cool-headed characters can have a deliciously dry wit and a flair for playful flirtation. There is something urbane about this placement. And you won't find a more responsible soul than Mercury Capricorn.

MERCURY CAPRICORN COMBINATIONS

Mercury Capricorn / Mercury Capricorn

♑ ♑

When you put two such determined and goal-oriented thinkers together, they will probably spend a lot of time figuring out ways to achieve, bring their plans to fruition, and likely, make money. Both have excellent powers of concentration, and once they make up their minds to go for something, their heads are down and off they go. In these ways, this pairing makes for a wonderful partnership at work, for setting and meeting the big goals in romantic relationships (such as saving for a home), and for collaborating on projects with friends. Since neither is naturally spontaneous, they will never speak until they have really thought about how they want to express their thoughts. They are not big communicators, unless they have something to say. Most of the time, these two are content sitting next to each other reading books in silence. Being so levelheaded and methodical, other Mercury placements might find them a little boring. When two Mercury Capricorns meet up, however, they are content to have another soul who understands how important it is to be persistent and practical.

Mercury Capricorn / Mercury Aquarius

♑ ♒

Mercury Capricorns can be steadfast and überpractical in their thinking. Some might even call them a bit repressed or old-fashioned. There is a definite seriousness to how they like things to be discussed. A Mercury Capricorn person can seem very controlling to others. When you put Mercury Aquarius in a relationship with Mercury Capricorn, it will sometimes feel like a drill sergeant (Mercury Capricorn) is hanging out with a hippie (Mercury Aquarius). Mercury Aquarius couldn't care less about anything too straight-laced. They like to live in the moment and are open to any and all possibilities, whereas Mercury Capricorn likes to think everything through and make a cogent decision based on facts. Mercury Aquarius thinks most facts are not really accurate, and they are willing to explore to figure things out. Opposites do sometimes attract, and these two could have a unique relationship. It will either be totally upsetting or completely energizing. The secret formula for success here is to realize that both could use a little dose of how the other one sees the world.

Mercury Capricorn / Mercury Pisces

♑ ♓

Being a water sign, Mercury Pisces does best when around people who can hold space for them: just as a lake is held by the earth or a clay jar holds water, there is something nice when the element of water meets the element of earth. Since Mercury Capricorn is as earthy as it gets, these two fit well together. The difficulty arises from the fact that Mercury Capricorn sometimes lacks imagination because they get so caught up in their practical thinking processes. They sometimes forget the importance of taking a day off and allowing the mind to daydream. Mercury Pisces, on the other hand, is the king or queen of daydreaming. When Mercury Pisces's excessive dreaminess gets them into trouble, however, Mercury Capricorn is able to step in and bring order to chaos. Mercury Capricorn can erect the scaffolding around those Mercury Pisces visions, giving them the structure they need to flourish. If Mercury Capricorn wants life to be a little more sparkly and realizes that working all the time is pretty boring, then Mercury Pisces will be the perfect person to help them escape from the doldrums. Mercury Pisces will enjoy opening Mercury Capricorn to the joys of the unseen world. Mercury Capricorn's addiction to order and routine will melt away under Mercury Pisces's influence. The steady grasp on reality, possessed by Mercury Capricorn, will bring great security to Mercury Pisces. This combination supplies the missing links which the other lacks.

MERCURY AQUARIUS

AQUARIUS IS THE MOST INHERENTLY OPEN OF ALL
the zodiac signs, with the least tendency toward bias—they
approach the world from a neutral position. They accept situations for what they are and people for who they are. Both
sides of an argument can be heard, and Mercury Aquarius
will resist picking a side. A person with Mercury in Aquarius can pretty much communicate with anyone, since they
are not prone to passing judgment. They abide by the mot-
tos "To each his own" and "Live and let live." They are patently clear about the importance of hearing all viewpoints.
They are obsessed with freedom of speech, thought, and action. Humanitarians to the core, they are always dreaming
of a better world. Their thoughts center on how to improve
the human condition. They make excellent innovators,
politicians, and scientists. If there is a new electronic gad-

get, they will be first in line to buy one. They often see the worth of an invention long before other people see its value. Their minds are focused on the world of possibilities, in whatever field they are in. Rarely do they obsess about the past. The future is what calls their attention. Exposure to other cultures and alternate realities nourishes them mentally. Their curious minds need to be fed with all matter of topics, and the more bizarre and eccentric the better for Mercury Aquarius. Their communication style is somewhat detached and very objective. If you want someone to communicate a difficult message, they will have the ability to convey what needs to be said in a cool and clear style. The irrational world of intense emotions is not their thing. If you get too emotional with them, they may cock their heads and look at you as if you are from another planet. Mercury Aquarius does best when they can creatively supply solutions to difficult problems; however, they are not always superpractical. Sometimes their ideas are pretty random and not entirely thought through. They are keen on how things can be better, but they sometimes forget to check all the practical ways that their ideas need to be implemented to succeed. Their minds can be so oriented toward the future that they struggle with being present. These progressive thinkers are all about originality. Since Aquarius is the sign that governs astrology, they have a natural ability to understand the complexities of reading an astrology chart.

MERCURY AQUARIUS COMBINATIONS

These two share the same philosophical approach to life. Intellectual topics fascinate Mercury Aquarius. They excel at brainstorming together and find real enjoyment spending hours thinking up ways to improve anything, whether it's raising money for a nonprofit they both believe in or redesigning the kitchen. One thing is for sure: they are both such completely original thinkers they will never bore one another. All day long, their brilliant and ingenious minds will delight in challenging each other's ideas and concepts. Rarely will they argue, but they might take turns accusing the other of being too fanatical once in a while. When they put their minds together, there is no telling what their iconoclastic brains will come up with. Sometimes they are both just downright quirky, at other times eccentric, and often just plain outrageous. This pair inspires others to think, "I wish I had the nerve to be as 'out there' as they are"—at least in the thinking department! There is something revolutionary and rebellious about this potent combination. The status quo is never of much interest to Mercury Aquarius. They believe in living a bit on the edge. When two Mercury Aquarians team up, the result is never mundane.

Mercury Aquarius / Mercury Pisces

Mercury Aquarius has a mind that is focused on the mental and intellectual side of life. Mercury Pisces has a mind that operates from the world of intuition. Mercury Pisces might try to read into that swirling, complex Aquarian mind, but they will probably feel as if they have been caught in a tornado and dumped in Oz. Mercury Aquarius's brain likes to rove all over the place, encountering new ideas and testing their beliefs. Their minds are spacious, and they like to focus on the big picture. Mercury Pisces is more about sympathetic and empathetic reasoning and connecting at a sensitive level. In the beginning, these two might think they are quite similar because both are a bit unconventional, but their intellectual and communication styles are profoundly different. Mercury Aquarius is detached. They have a cool and calm speaking style, but they are gentle to the core. Mercury Pisces is emotional; when they talk about something they really believe in, they might even get teary because they care so much. The key to success with this combination is to find the flow between their styles. They could exchange big life lessons that would be valuable to both individuals. Mercury Pisces could stand some exposure to abstract thinking minus the emotions. And Mercury Aquarius would be smart to learn the value of imbuing mental investments with an emotional connection.

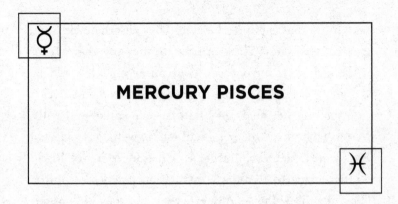

MERCURY PISCES

PISCES IS A WATER SIGN—EMOTIONALLY SENSITIVE and deeply intuitive. Mercury Pisces is so attuned to the nuances and subtleties of how others communicate and how the world delivers information that it can often seem like they are on the verge of a trance. Their minds are comfortable in the realm of the unconscious. With their preference for following their imagination into the world of dreams rather than focusing on the mundane realities of daily life, it is no wonder that Mercury Pisces is considered a creative placement. Others might find them a bit absentminded and a little "out of touch," but they are really just in a different mental zone than the other zodiac signs. In fact, they prefer the world of fantasy because their sensitive nature often finds the real world a little too harsh. Mercury Pisces has a mind that is impressionable. They absorb quickly and respond intuitively. These are the mimics and chameleons of the zodiac. If anyone can copy an accent, it would be Mercury Pisces. Sometimes they are a little too sensitive. If their feelings get hurt, they will become sullen and withdrawn. Their minds do not handle stress well. Peace is what they want to achieve, and for this reason, Mercury Pisces is often attracted to a daily meditation practice or prayer. They like to see the good in everyone, but they are not terribly great at spotting when someone might be harmful. They might see a red flag in someone's behavior but are likely to convince themselves it's only pink, simply because they want to believe everything is really just fine. Mercury Pisces lives in an enchanted world of their own creation— but they need to realize that trolls and goblins live in magic forests, alongside the unicorns and fairies.

MERCURY PISCES COMBINATIONS

Mercury Pisces / Mercury Pisces

♓ ♓

Communication between two Mercury Pisces can feel almost telepathic. Both are highly empathetic; they are so attuned to each other's emotions that they can and often will carry each other's burdens and joys. There is a great capacity for compassion with this combination. Their psychic antennas are fully up when they hang out together. The beauty of this match is the totally dreamlike quality of their minds melting into each other. There is a feeling of coming home, as the two of them fuse together at the level of mental processing. Both are mystical and interested in yoga, art, metaphysics, and anything that has to do with understanding the world at a deeper and more spiritual level. They both seek to hide from the harsh and coarse aspects of life. Others might find this pair exasperatingly vague at times and seeming to lack common sense. Their powers of reasoning are not obvious; they operate at an intuitive level. These two have a tremendous capacity for picking up all the subtle nuances that others miss, and that Piscean influence compels them to rely mainly on inner feelings rather than intellect. This can be a problem when they are faced with the inevitable conflicts that are part of all relationships. These two would rather avoid disagreements, which can lead to resentments and failures of communication that grow worse over time. A desire to escape can also lead to self-medicating through drugs and alcohol. This is dangerous to the self, of course, but also detrimental to relationships professional and personal. The trick is for both of them to realize that if they keep themselves pure in body, mind, and spirit, they are more able to connect with a higher consciousness. So they must guard against anything that helps them escape in a negative way and instead turn to music, art, and Mother Nature.

MERCURY TABLES

1930–2019

HOW TO USE THE
MERCURY TABLES

DATE	MOTION	SIGN
Date of motion or sign change	D for *direct* motion R$_x$ for *retrograde* motion	Mercury sign

1. Find your year of birth, located at the top of each page.

2. If you do not see your actual birthday listed, please look for the closest date *before* your birthday.

3. Mercury changes signs quite often, as well as direction. You will see on these tables that Mercury is either going to be in *direct* motion or *retrograde* motion. Again, take note that for the dates not listed, the previous date indicates the Mercury condition until the next given date.

4. Without doing a more precise calculation of a Mercury placement (based on exact time and place of birth), these tables are just meant to be used as a guideline. If the date you are looking up falls on a date where the direction or sign changes, you have to look at both the entry listed and the one before. When you read both descriptions, you will get a better sense of which one feels more accurate.

5. I based these Mercury tables on Eastern Standard Time zone. If Mercury changed signs late in the day, I left it with the previous sign since most of that day Mercury was still hanging out there.

6. Since time and place are so important to a *precise* Mercury calculation, I strongly suggest using the Mercury calculator found at www.lunarium.co.uk/moonsign/mercury.jsp.

1930

DATE	MOTION	SIGN
January 1	D	Capricorn
January 2	D	Aquarius
January 13	R_x	Aquarius
January 23	R_x	Capricorn
February 2	D	Capricorn
February 15	D	Aquarius
March 10	D	Pisces
March 27	D	Aries
April 10	D	Taurus
May 1	D	Gemini
May 9	R_x	Gemini
May 17	R_x	Taurus
June 1	D	Taurus
June 15	D	Gemini
July 5	D	Cancer
July 19	D	Leo
August 4	D	Virgo
August 26	D	Libra
September 8	R_x	Libra
September 20	R_x	Virgo
October 1	D	Virgo
October 11	D	Libra
October 29	D	Scorpio
November 17	D	Sagittarius
December 7	D	Capricorn
December 28	R_x	Capricorn

1931

DATE	MOTION	SIGN
January 17	D	Capricorn
February 11	D	Aquarius
March 2	D	Pisces
March 19	D	Aries
April 3	D	Taurus
April 20	R$_x$	Taurus
May 13	D	Taurus
June 11	D	Gemini
June 26	D	Cancer
July 11	D	Leo
July 29	D	Virgo
August 22	R$_x$	Virgo
September 14	D	Virgo
October 4	D	Libra
October 22	D	Scorpio
November 10	D	Sagittarius
December 2	D	Capricorn
December 12	R$_x$	Capricorn
December 20	R$_x$	Sagittarius
December 31	D	Sagittarius

1932

DATE	MOVEMENT	SIGN
January 14	D	Capricorn
February 5	D	Aquarius
February 23	D	Pisces
March 10	D	Aries
March 31	R_x	Aries
April 24	D	Aries
May 16	D	Taurus
June 3	D	Gemini
June 17	D	Cancer
July 2	D	Leo
July 28	D	Virgo
August 3	R_x	Virgo
August 10	R_x	Leo
August 27	D	Leo
September 9	D	Virgo
September 26	D	Libra
October 13	D	Scorpio
November 3	D	Sagittarius
November 24	R_x	Sagittarius
December 14	D	Sagittarius

DATE	MOTION	SIGN
January 8	D	Capricorn
January 28	D	Aquarius
February 14	D	Pisces
March 3	D	Aries
March 14	R_x	Aries
March 26	R_x	Pisces
April 6	D	Pisces
April 17	D	Aries
May 10	D	Taurus
May 25	D	Gemini
June 8	D	Cancer
June 27	D	Leo
July 16	R_x	Leo
August 9	D	Leo
September 2	D	Virgo
September 18	D	Libra
October 6	D	Scorpio
October 30	D	Sagittarius
November 8	R_x	Sagittarius
November 16	R_x	Scorpio
November 28	D	Scorpio
December 12	D	Sagittarius

1934

DATE	MOTION	SIGN
January 1	D	Capricorn
January 20	D	Aquarius
February 6	D	Pisces
February 24	R_x	Pisces
March 19	D	Pisces
April 15	D	Aries
May 2	D	Taurus
May 17	D	Gemini
June 1	D	Cancer
June 27	R_x	Cancer
July 22	D	Cancer
August 9	D	Leo
August 25	D	Virgo
September 10	D	Libra
September 30	D	Scorpio
October 23	R_x	Scorpio
November 12	D	Scorpio
December 6	D	Sagittarius
December 25	D	Capricorn

DATE	MOTION	SIGN
January 13	D	Aquarius
February 1	D	Pisces
February 8	R$_x$	Pisces
February 15	R$_x$	Aquarius
March 2	D	Aquarius
March 19	D	Pisces
April 8	D	Aries
April 24	D	Taurus
May 8	D	Gemini
May 30	D	Cancer
June 8	R$_x$	Cancer
June 20	R$_x$	Gemini
July 3	D	Cancer
July 14	D	Cancer
August 2	D	Leo
August 17	D	Virgo
September 3	D	Libra
September 28	D	Scorpio
October 5	R$_x$	Scorpio
October 11	R$_x$	Libra
October 26	D	Libra
November 10	D	Scorpio
November 29	D	Sagittarius
December 18	D	Capricorn

1936

DATE	MOTION	SIGN
January 6	D	Aquarius
January 22	R_x	Aquarius
February 12	D	Aquarius
March 12	D	Pisces
March 30	D	Pisces
April 15	D	Taurus
May 1	D	Gemini
May 19	R_x	Gemini
June 12	D	Gemini
July 9	D	Cancer
July 23	D	Leo
August 8	D	Virgo
August 27	D	Libra
September 17	R_x	Libra
October 9	D	Libra
November 2	D	Scorpio
November 21	D	Sagittarius
December 10	D	Capricorn

1937

DATE	MOTION	SIGN
January 1	D	Aquarius
January 6	R$_x$	Aquarius
January 10	R$_x$	Capricorn
January 26	D	Capricorn
February 14	D	Aquarius
March 6	D	Pisces
March 23	D	Aries
April 7	D	Taurus
April 30	R$_x$	Taurus
May 24	D	Taurus
June 14	D	Gemini
July 1	D	Cancer
July 15	D	Leo
August 1	D	Virgo
September 1	R$_x$	Virgo
September 23	D	Virgo
October 8	D	Libra
October 26	D	Scorpio
November 13	D	Sagittarius
December 4	D	Capricorn
December 21	R$_x$	Capricorn

1938

DATE	MOTION	SIGN
January 7	R$_x$	Sagittarius
January 10	D	Sagittarius
January 13	D	Capricorn
February 8	D	Aquarius
February 27	D	Pisces
March 15	D	Aries
April 1	D	Taurus
April 11	R$_x$	Taurus
April 23	R$_x$	Aries
May 5	D	Aries
May 16	D	Taurus
June 8	D	Gemini
June 22	D	Cancer
July 7	D	Leo
July 27	D	Virgo
August 14	R$_x$	Virgo
September 3	R$_x$	Leo
September 7	D	Leo
September 10	D	Virgo
October 1	D	Libra
October 18	D	Scorpio
November 7	D	Sagittarius
December 4	R$_x$	Sagittarius
December 24	D	Sagittarius

1939

DATE	MOTION	SIGN
January 12	D	Capricorn
February 1	D	Aquarius
February 19	D	Pisces
March 7	D	Aries
March 24	R$_x$	Aries
April 16	D	Aries
May 14	D	Taurus
May 31	D	Gemini
June 14	D	Cancer
June 30	D	Leo
July 27	R$_x$	Leo
August 20	D	Leo
September 7	D	Virgo
September 23	D	Libra
October 11	D	Scorpio
November 1	D	Sagittarius
November 18	R$_x$	Sagittarius
December 3	R$_x$	Scorpio
December 8	D	Scorpio
December 13	D	Sagittarius

1940

DATE	MOTION	SIGN
January 6	D	Capricorn
January 25	D	Aquarius
February 11	D	Pisces
March 4	D	Aries
March 6	R$_x$	Aries
March 8	R$_x$	Pisces
March 29	D	Pisces
April 17	D	Aries
May 7	D	Taurus
May 21	D	Gemini
June 5	D	Cancer
June 26	D	Leo
July 8	R$_x$	Leo
July 21	R$_x$	Cancer
August 1	D	Cancer
August 11	D	Leo
August 29	D	Virgo
September 14	D	Libra
October 3	D	Scorpio
October 31	R$_x$	Scorpio
November 21	D	Scorpio
December 9	D	Sagittarius
December 29	D	Capricorn

1941

DATE	MOTION	SIGN
January 17	D	Aquarius
February 3	D	Pisces
February 17	R_x	Pisces
March 7	R_x	Aquarius
March 11	D	Aquarius
March 16	D	Pisces
April 12	D	Aries
April 29	D	Taurus
May 13	D	Gemini
May 29	D	Cancer
June 20	R_x	Cancer
July 14	D	Cancer
August 6	D	Leo
August 21	D	Virgo
September 7	D	Libra
September 28	D	Scorpio
October 15	R_x	Scorpio
October 30	R_x	Libra
November 5	D	Libra
November 12	D	Scorpio
December 3	D	Sagittarius
December 22	D	Capricorn

1942

DATE	MOTION	SIGN
January 9	D	Aquarius
February 1	R$_x$	Aquarius
February 22	D	Aquarius
March 17	D	Pisces
April 5	D	Aries
April 20	D	Taurus
May 5	D	Gemini
May 31	R$_x$	Gemini
June 24	D	Gemini
July 13	D	Cancer
July 29	D	Leo
August 13	D	Virgo
August 31	D	Libra
September 28	R$_x$	Libra
October 20	D	Libra
November 7	D	Scorpio
November 26	D	Sagittarius
December 15	D	Capricorn

1943

DATE	MOTION	SIGN
January 3	D	Aquarius
January 16	R$_x$	Aquarius
January 28	R$_x$	Capricorn
February 5	D	Capricorn
February 15	D	Aquarius
March 11	D	Pisces
March 28	D	Aries
April 12	D	Taurus
April 30	D	Gemini
May 12	R$_x$	Gemini
May 26	R$_x$	Taurus
June 5	D	Taurus
June 14	D	Gemini
July 6	D	Cancer
July 20	D	Leo
August 5	D	Virgo
August 27	D	Libra
September 11	R$_x$	Libra
September 25	R$_x$	Virgo
October 3	D	Virgo
October 12	D	Libra
October 31	D	Scorpio
November 18	D	Sagittarius
December 8	D	Capricorn
December 30	R$_x$	Capricorn

1944

DATE	MOTION	SIGN
January 20	D	Capricorn
February 12	D	Aquarius
March 3	D	Pisces
March 19	D	Aries
April 3	D	Taurus
April 22	R_x	Taurus
May 16	D	Taurus
June 11	D	Gemini
June 27	D	Cancer
July 11	D	Leo
July 29	D	Virgo
August 24	R_x	Virgo
September 16	D	Virgo
October 4	D	Libra
October 22	D	Scorpio
November 10	D	Sagittarius
December 1	D	Capricorn
December 13	R_x	Capricorn
December 24	R_x	Sagittarius

1945

DATE	MOTION	SIGN
January 2	D	Sagittarius
January 14	D	Capricorn
February 5	D	Aquarius
February 23	D	Pisces
March 11	D	Aries
April 3	R_x	Aries
April 27	D	Aries
May 16	D	Taurus
June 4	D	Gemini
June 18	D	Cancer
July 3	D	Leo
July 26	D	Virgo
August 6	R_x	Virgo
August 17	R_x	Leo
August 30	D	Leo
September 10	D	Virgo
September 27	D	Libra
October 15	D	Scorpio
November 4	D	Sagittarius
November 27	R_x	Sagittarius
December 17	D	Sagittarius

1946

DATE	MOTION	SIGN
January 9	D	Capricorn
January 29	D	Aquarius
February 15	D	Pisces
March 4	D	Aries
March 16	R_x	Aries
April 1	R_x	Pisces
April 9	D	Pisces
April 16	D	Aries
May 11	D	Taurus
May 27	D	Gemini
June 10	D	Cancer
June 28	D	Leo
July 19	R_x	Leo
August 13	D	Leo
September 3	D	Virgo
September 19	D	Libra
October 8	D	Scorpio
October 30	D	Sagittarius
November 11	R_x	Sagittarius
November 21	R_x	Scorpio
November 30	D	Scorpio
December 13	D	Sagittarius

1947

DATE	MOTION	SIGN
January 3	D	Capricorn
January 22	D	Aquarius
February 8	D	Pisces
February 27	R$_x$	Pisces
March 22	D	Pisces
April 16	D	Aries
May 4	D	Taurus
May 18	D	Gemini
June 2	D	Cancer
July 1	R$_x$	Cancer
July 25	D	Cancer
August 10	D	Leo
August 26	D	Virgo
September 12	D	Libra
October 1	D	Scorpio
October 25	R$_x$	Scorpio
November 15	D	Scorpio
December 7	D	Sagittarius
December 27	D	Capricorn

1948

DATE	MOTION	SIGN
January 14	D	Aquarius
February 2	D	Pisces
February 11	R$_x$	Pisces
February 20	R$_x$	Aquarius
March 4	D	Aquarius
March 18	D	Pisces
April 9	D	Aries
April 25	D	Taurus
May 9	D	Gemini
May 28	D	Cancer
June 11	R$_x$	Cancer
June 28	R$_x$	Gemini
July 5	D	Gemini
July 12	D	Cancer
August 2	D	Leo
August 17	D	Virgo
September 3	D	Libra
September 27	D	Scorpio
October 8	R$_x$	Scorpio
October 17	R$_x$	Libra
October 28	D	Libra
November 10	D	Scorpio
November 29	D	Sagittarius
December 18	D	Capricorn

1949

DATE	MOTION	SIGN
January 6	D	Aquarius
January 25	R_x	Aquarius
February 15	D	Aquarius
March 14	D	Pisces
April 1	D	Aries
April 16	D	Taurus
May 2	D	Gemini
May 23	R_x	Gemini
June 16	D	Gemini
July 10	D	Cancer
July 25	D	Leo
August 9	D	Virgo
August 28	D	Libra
September 21	R_x	Libra
October 13	D	Libra
November 3	D	Scorpio
November 22	D	Sagittarius
December 11	D	Capricorn

1950

DATE	MOTION	SIGN
January 1	D	Aquarius
January 8	R_x	Aquarius
January 15	R_x	Capricorn
January 28	D	Capricorn
February 14	D	Aquarius
March 8	D	Pisces
March 24	D	Aries
April 8	D	Taurus
May 3	R_x	Taurus
May 27	D	Taurus
June 14	D	Gemini
July 2	D	Cancer
July 16	D	Leo
August 2	D	Virgo
August 27	D	Libra
September 4	R_x	Libra
September 11	R_x	Virgo
September 26	D	Virgo
October 9	D	Libra
October 27	D	Scorpio
November 15	D	Sagittarius
December 5	D	Capricorn
December 23	R_x	Capricorn

1951

DATE	MOTION	SIGN
January 12	D	Capricorn
February 9	D	Aquarius
February 28	D	Pisces
March 16	D	Aries
April 2	D	Taurus
April 14	R_x	Taurus
May 2	R_x	Aries
May 8	D	Aries
May 15	D	Taurus
June 9	D	Gemini
June 24	D	Cancer
July 8	D	Leo
July 27	D	Virgo
August 17	R_x	Virgo
September 10	D	Virgo
October 2	D	Libra
October 20	D	Scorpio
November 8	D	Sagittarius
December 2	D	Capricorn
December 12	R_x	Sagittarius
December 27	D	Sagittarius

1952

DATE	MOTION	SIGN
January 13	D	Capricorn
February 3	D	Aquarius
February 20	D	Pisces
March 7	D	Aries
March 26	R$_x$	Aries
April 19	D	Aries
May 14	D	Taurus
May 31	D	Gemini
June 14	D	Cancer
June 30	D	Leo
July 30	R$_x$	Leo
August 22	D	Leo
September 7	D	Virgo
September 23	D	Libra
October 11	D	Scorpio
November 1	D	Sagittarius
November 20	R$_x$	Sagittarius
December 10	D	Sagittarius

1953

DATE	MOTION	SIGN
January 6	D	Capricorn
January 25	D	Aquarius
February 12	D	Pisces
March 2	D	Aries
March 9	R$_x$	Aries
March 16	R$_x$	Pisces
March 31	D	Pisces
April 17	D	Aries
May 8	D	Taurus
May 23	D	Gemini
June 6	D	Cancer
June 26	D	Leo
July 11	R$_x$	Leo
July 28	R$_x$	Cancer
August 5	D	Cancer
August 11	D	Leo
August 31	D	Virgo
September 16	D	Libra
October 4	D	Scorpio
October 31	D	Sagittarius
November 4	R$_x$	Sagittarius
November 7	R$_x$	Scorpio
November 24	D	Scorpio
December 10	D	Sagittarius
December 30	D	Capricorn

1954

DATE	MOTION	SIGN
January 18	D	Aquarius
February 4	D	Pisces
February 20	R$_x$	Pisces
March 14	D	Pisces
April 13	D	Aries
April 30	D	Taurus
May 14	D	Gemini
May 30	D	Cancer
June 24	R$_x$	Cancer
July 17	D	Cancer
August 7	D	Leo
August 22	D	Virgo
September 8	D	Libra
September 29	D	Scorpio
October 18	R$_x$	Scorpio
November 4	R$_x$	Libra
November 8	D	Libra
November 11	D	Scorpio
December 4	D	Sagittarius
December 23	D	Capricorn

1955

DATE	MOTION	SIGN
January 11	D	Aquarius
February 4	R$_x$	Aquarius
February 25	D	Aquarius
March 17	D	Pisces
April 6	D	Aries
April 22	D	Taurus
May 6	D	Gemini
June 4	R$_x$	Gemini
June 28	D	Gemini
July 13	D	Cancer
July 30	D	Leo
August 14	D	Virgo
September 1	D	Libra
October 1	R$_x$	Libra
October 23	D	Libra
November 8	D	Scorpio
November 27	D	Sagittarius
December 16	D	Capricorn

DATE	MOTION	SIGN
January 4	D	Aquarius
January 18	R_x	Aquarius
February 2	R_x	Capricorn
February 8	D	Capricorn
February 15	D	Aquarius
March 11	D	Pisces
March 29	D	Aries
April 12	D	Taurus
April 30	D	Gemini
May 14	R_x	Gemini
June 7	D	Gemini
July 6	D	Cancer
July 21	D	Leo
August 5	D	Virgo
August 26	D	Libra
September 13	R_x	Libra
September 29	R_x	Virgo
October 5	D	Virgo
October 11	D	Libra
October 31	D	Scorpio
November 18	D	Sagittarius
December 8	D	Capricorn

DATE	MOTION	SIGN
January 1	R$_x$	Capricorn
January 22	D	Capricorn
February 12	D	Aquarius
March 4	D	Pisces
March 20	D	Aries
April 5	D	Taurus
April 25	R$_x$	Taurus
May 19	D	Taurus
June 12	D	Gemini
June 28	D	Cancer
July 12	D	Leo
July 30	D	Virgo
August 27	R$_x$	Virgo
September 19	D	Virgo
October 6	D	Libra
October 23	D	Scorpio
November 11	D	Sagittarius
December 2	D	Capricorn
December 16	R$_x$	Capricorn
December 28	R$_x$	Sagittarius

1958

DATE	MOTION	SIGN
January 5	D	Sagittarius
January 14	D	Capricorn
February 6	D	Aquarius
February 24	D	Pisces
March 12	D	Aries
April 2	D	Taurus
April 6	R$_x$	Taurus
April 10	R$_x$	Aries
April 30	D	Aries
May 17	D	Taurus
June 5	D	Gemini
June 20	D	Cancer
July 5	D	Leo
July 26	D	Virgo
August 9	R$_x$	Virgo
August 23	R$_x$	Leo
September 2	D	Leo
September 11	D	Virgo
September 29	D	Libra
October 16	D	Scorpio
November 5	D	Sagittarius
November 30	R$_x$	Sagittarius
December 20	D	Sagittarius

1959

DATE	MOTION	SIGN
January 10	D	Capricorn
January 30	D	Aquarius
February 17	D	Pisces
March 5	D	Aries
March 19	R$_x$	Aries
April 12	D	Aries
May 12	D	Taurus
May 28	D	Gemini
June 11	D	Cancer
June 28	D	Leo
July 23	R$_x$	Leo
August 16	D	Leo
September 5	D	Virgo
September 21	D	Libra
October 9	D	Scorpio
October 31	D	Sagittarius
November 14	R$_x$	Sagittarius
November 25	R$_x$	Scorpio
December 4	D	Scorpio
December 13	D	Sagittarius

1960

DATE	MOTION	SIGN
January 4	D	Capricorn
January 23	D	Aquarius
February 9	D	Pisces
March 1	R$_x$	Pisces
March 24	D	Pisces
April 16	D	Aries
May 4	D	Taurus
May 19	D	Gemini
June 2	D	Cancer
July 1	D	Leo
July 3	R$_x$	Leo
July 6	R$_x$	Cancer
July 27	D	Cancer
August 10	D	Leo
August 27	D	Virgo
September 12	D	Libra
October 1	D	Scorpio
October 27	R$_x$	Scorpio
November 17	D	Scorpio
December 7	D	Sagittarius
December 27	D	Capricorn

1961

DATE	MOTION	SIGN
January 14	D	Aquarius
February 1	D	Pisces
February 13	R_x	Pisces
February 24	R_x	Aquarius
March 7	D	Aquarius
March 18	D	Pisces
April 10	D	Aries
April 26	D	Taurus
May 10	D	Gemini
May 28	D	Cancer
June 14	R_x	Cancer
July 9	D	Cancer
August 4	D	Leo
August 18	D	Virgo
September 5	D	Libra
September 27	D	Scorpio
October 11	R_x	Scorpio
October 22	R_x	Libra
October 31	D	Libra
November 11	D	Scorpio
December 1	D	Sagittarius
December 20	D	Capricorn

1962

DATE	MOTION	SIGN
January 7	D	Aquarius
January 27	R$_x$	Aquarius
February 18	D	Aquarius
March 15	D	Pisces
April 3	D	Aries
April 18	D	Taurus
May 3	D	Gemini
May 26	R$_x$	Gemini
June 19	D	Gemini
July 11	D	Cancer
July 26	D	Leo
August 10	D	Virgo
August 29	D	Libra
September 24	R$_x$	Libra
October 15	D	Libra
November 5	D	Scorpio
November 23	D	Sagittarius
December 12	D	Capricorn

1963

DATE	MOTION	SIGN
January 2	D	Aquarius
January 11	R$_x$	Aquarius
January 20	R$_x$	Capricorn
February 1	D	Capricorn
February 15	D	Aquarius
March 9	D	Pisces
March 26	D	Aries
April 10	D	Taurus
May 3	D	Gemini
May 7	R$_x$	Gemini
May 10	R$_x$	Taurus
May 30	D	Taurus
June 15	D	Gemini
July 4	D	Cancer
July 18	D	Leo
August 3	D	Virgo
August 26	D	Libra
September 7	R$_x$	Libra
September 16	R$_x$	Virgo
September 29	D	Virgo
October 10	D	Libra
October 28	D	Scorpio
November 16	D	Sagittarius
December 6	D	Capricorn
December 26	R$_x$	Capricorn

1964

DATE	MOTION	SIGN
January 15	D	Capricorn
February 11	D	Aquarius
March 1	D	Pisces
March 17	D	Aries
April 2	D	Taurus
April 17	R_x	Taurus
May 10	D	Taurus
June 9	D	Gemini
June 24	D	Cancer
July 9	D	Leo
July 27	D	Virgo
August 19	R_x	Virgo
September 11	D	Virgo
October 3	D	Libra
October 20	D	Scorpio
November 8	D	Sagittarius
December 1	D	Capricorn
December 9	R_x	Capricorn
December 16	R_x	Sagittarius
December 29	D	Sagittarius

1965

DATE	MOTION	SIGN
January 13	D	Capricorn
February 3	D	Aquarius
February 21	D	Pisces
March 9	D	Aries
March 29	R_x	Aries
April 22	D	Aries
May 15	D	Taurus
June 2	D	Gemini
June 16	D	Cancer
July 1	D	Leo
July 31	D	Virgo
August 2	R_x	Virgo
August 3	R_x	Leo
August 25	D	Leo
September 8	D	Virgo
September 25	D	Libra
October 13	D	Scorpio
November 2	D	Sagittarius
November 23	R_x	Sagittarius
December 13	D	Sagittarius

1966

DATE	MOTION	SIGN
January 7	D	Capricorn
January 27	D	Aquarius
February 13	D	Pisces
March 3	D	Aries
March 12	R$_x$	Aries
March 22	R$_x$	Pisces
April 4	D	Pisces
April 18	D	Aries
May 9	D	Taurus
May 24	D	Gemini
June 7	D	Cancer
June 27	D	Leo
July 15	R$_x$	Leo
August 8	D	Leo
September 1	D	Virgo
September 17	D	Libra
October 6	D	Scorpio
October 30	D	Sagittarius
November 6	R$_x$	Sagittarius
November 13	R$_x$	Scorpio
November 26	D	Scorpio
December 11	D	Sagittarius

1967

DATE	MOTION	SIGN
January 1	D	Capricorn
January 19	D	Aquarius
February 6	D	Pisces
February 23	R_x	Pisces
March 17	D	Pisces
April 14	D	Aries
May 2	D	Taurus
May 16	D	Gemini
May 31	D	Cancer
June 26	R_x	Cancer
July 20	D	Cancer
August 9	D	Leo
August 24	D	Virgo
September 9	D	Libra
September 30	D	Scorpio
October 21	R_x	Scorpio
November 10	D	Scorpio
December 5	D	Sagittarius
December 24	D	Capricorn

DATE	MOTION	SIGN
January 12	D	Aquarius
February 1	D	Pisces
February 6	R_x	Pisces
February 11	R_x	Aquarius
February 28	D	Aquarius
March 17	D	Pisces
April 7	D	Aries
April 22	D	Taurus
May 7	D	Gemini
May 30	D	Cancer
June 6	R_x	Cancer
June 14	R_x	Gemini
June 30	D	Gemini
July 13	D	Cancer
July 31	D	Leo
August 15	D	Virgo
September 1	D	Libra
September 28	D	Scorpio
October 3	R_x	Scorpio
October 8	R_x	Libra
October 24	D	Libra
November 8	D	Scorpio
November 27	D	Sagittarius
December 16	D	Capricorn

1969

DATE	MOTION	SIGN
January 4	D	Aquarius
January 20	R$_x$	Aquarius
February 10	D	Aquarius
March 12	D	Pisces
March 30	D	Aries
April 14	D	Taurus
April 30	D	Gemini
May 18	R$_x$	Gemini
June 10	D	Gemini
July 8	D	Cancer
July 23	D	Leo
August 7	D	Virgo
August 27	D	Libra
September 16	R$_x$	Libra
October 7	R$_x$	Virgo
October 9	D	Libra
November 1	D	Scorpio
November 20	D	Sagittarius
December 9	D	Capricorn

1970

DATE	MOTION	SIGN
January 4	R$_x$	Aquarius
January 24	D	Capricorn
February 13	D	Aquarius
March 5	D	Pisces
March 22	D	Aries
April 6	D	Taurus
April 28	R$_x$	Taurus
May 22	D	Taurus
June 13	D	Gemini
June 30	D	Cancer
July 14	D	Leo
July 31	D	Virgo
August 30	R$_x$	Virgo
September 22	D	Virgo
October 7	D	Libra
October 25	D	Scorpio
November 13	D	Sagittarius
December 3	D	Capricorn
December 19	R$_x$	Capricorn

1971

DATE	MOTION	SIGN
January 3	R_x	Sagittarius
January 8	D	Sagittarius
January 14	D	Capricorn
February 8	D	Aquarius
February 26	D	Pisces
March 14	D	Aries
April 1	D	Taurus
April 9	R_x	Taurus
April 19	R_x	Aries
May 3	D	Aries
May 17	D	Taurus
June 7	D	Gemini
June 21	D	Cancer
July 6	D	Leo
July 26	D	Virgo
August 13	R_x	Virgo
August 30	R_x	Leo
September 5	D	Leo
September 11	D	Virgo
September 30	D	Libra
October 17	D	Scorpio
November 6	D	Sagittarius
December 3	R_x	Sagittarius
December 23	D	Sagittarius

1972

DATE	MOTION	SIGN
January 11	D	Capricorn
February 1	D	Aquarius
February 18	D	Pisces
March 5	D	Aries
March 21	R$_x$	Aries
April 14	D	Aries
May 13	D	Taurus
May 29	D	Gemini
June 12	D	Cancer
June 28	D	Leo
July 25	R$_x$	Leo
August 18	D	Leo
September 5	D	Virgo
September 21	D	Libra
October 9	D	Scorpio
October 30	D	Sagittarius
November 16	R$_x$	Sagittarius
November 29	R$_x$	Scorpio
December 13	D	Sagittarius

DATE	MOTION	SIGN
January 4	D	Capricorn
January 23	D	Aquarius
February 9	D	Pisces
March 4	R_x	Pisces
March 27	D	Pisces
April 16	D	Aries
May 6	D	Taurus
May 20	D	Gemini
June 4	D	Cancer
June 27	D	Leo
July 6	R_x	Leo
July 16	R_x	Cancer
July 31	D	Cancer
August 11	D	Leo
August 28	D	Virgo
September 13	D	Libra
October 3	D	Scorpio
October 30	R_x	Scorpio
November 19	D	Scorpio
December 9	D	Sagittarius
December 28	D	Capricorn

1974

DATE	MOTION	SIGN
January 16	D	Aquarius
February 3	D	Pisces
February 16	R_x	Pisces
March 2	R_x	Aquarius
March 10	D	Aquarius
March 18	D	Pisces
April 11	D	Aries
April 28	D	Taurus
May 12	D	Gemini
May 29	D	Cancer
June 18	R_x	Cancer
July 12	D	Cancer
August 5	D	Leo
August 20	D	Virgo
September 6	D	Libra
September 28	D	Scorpio
October 14	R_x	Scorpio
October 27	R_x	Libra
November 3	D	Libra
November 11	D	Scorpio
December 2	D	Sagittarius
December 21	D	Capricorn

1975

DATE	MOTION	SIGN
January 9	D	Aquarius
January 30	R$_x$	Aquarius
February 21	D	Aquarius
March 16	D	Pisces
April 4	D	Aries
April 19	D	Taurus
May 4	D	Gemini
May 29	R$_x$	Gemini
June 22	D	Gemini
July 12	D	Cancer
July 28	D	Leo
August 12	D	Virgo
August 30	D	Libra
September 27	R$_x$	Libra
October 18	D	Libra
November 6	D	Scorpio
November 25	D	Sagittarius
December 14	D	Capricorn

1976

DATE	MOTION	SIGN
January 3	D	Aquarius
January 14	R_x	Aquarius
January 25	R_x	Capricorn
February 4	D	Capricorn
February 15	D	Aquarius
March 9	D	Pisces
March 26	D	Aries
April 10	D	Taurus
April 30	D	Gemini
May 9	R_x	Gemini
May 20	R_x	Taurus
June 2	D	Taurus
June 14	D	Gemini
July 4	D	Cancer
July 18	D	Leo
August 3	D	Virgo
August 26	D	Libra
September 21	R_x	Virgo
October 1	D	Virgo
October 10	D	Libra
October 29	D	Scorpio
November 16	D	Sagittarius
December 6	D	Capricorn
December 28	R_x	Capricorn

1977

DATE	MOTION	SIGN
January 17	D	Capricorn
February 11	D	Aquarius
March 2	D	Pisces
March 18	D	Aries
April 3	D	Taurus
April 20	R_x	Taurus
May 14	D	Taurus
June 11	D	Gemini
June 26	D	Cancer
July 10	D	Leo
July 28	D	Virgo
August 22	R_x	Virgo
September 14	D	Virgo
October 4	D	Libra
October 21	D	Scorpio
November 9	D	Sagittarius
December 1	D	Capricorn
December 12	R_x	Capricorn
December 21	R_x	Sagittarius

1978

DATE	MOTION	SIGN
January 1	D	Sagittarius
January 14	D	Capricorn
February 4	D	Aquarius
February 22	D	Pisces
March 10	D	Aries
April 1	R$_x$	Aries
April 25	D	Aries
May 16	D	Taurus
June 3	D	Gemini
June 17	D	Cancer
July 3	D	Leo
July 27	D	Virgo
August 5	R$_x$	Virgo
August 13	R$_x$	Leo
September 9	D	Virgo
September 26	D	Libra
October 14	D	Scorpio
November 3	D	Sagittarius
November 26	R$_x$	Sagittarius
December 15	D	Sagittarius

1979

DATE	MOTION	SIGN
January 9	D	Capricorn
January 28	D	Aquarius
February 15	D	Pisces
March 4	D	Aries
March 15	R_x	Aries
March 28	R_x	Pisces
April 7	D	Pisces
April 17	D	Aries
May 11	D	Taurus
May 26	D	Gemini
June 9	D	Cancer
June 27	D	Leo
July 18	R_x	Leo
August 11	D	Leo
September 3	D	Virgo
September 18	D	Libra
October 7	D	Scorpio
October 30	D	Sagittarius
November 9	R_x	Sagittarius
November 18	R_x	Scorpio
November 29	D	Scorpio
December 12	D	Sagittarius

DATE	MOTION	SIGN
January 2	D	Capricorn
January 21	D	Aquarius
February 7	D	Pisces
February 26	R_x	Pisces
March 19	D	Pisces
April 14	D	Aries
May 2	D	Taurus
May 16	D	Gemini
June 1	D	Cancer
June 28	R_x	Cancer
July 22	D	Cancer
August 9	D	Leo
August 24	D	Virgo
September 10	D	Libra
September 30	D	Scorpio
October 23	R_x	Scorpio
November 12	D	Scorpio
December 5	D	Sagittarius
December 25	D	Capricorn

1981

DATE	MOTION	SIGN
January 12	D	Aquarius
January 31	D	Pisces
February 8	R$_x$	Pisces
February 16	R$_x$	Aquarius
March 2	D	Aquarius
March 18	D	Pisces
April 8	D	Aries
April 24	D	Taurus
May 8	D	Gemini
May 28	D	Cancer
June 9	R$_x$	Cancer
June 23	R$_x$	Gemini
July 3	D	Gemini
July 13	D	Cancer
August 1	D	Leo
August 16	D	Virgo
September 3	D	Libra
September 27	D	Scorpio
October 6	R$_x$	Scorpio
October 14	R$_x$	Libra
October 27	D	Libra
November 9	D	Scorpio
November 29	D	Sagittarius
December 18	D	Capricorn

1982

DATE	MOTION	SIGN
January 5	D	Aquarius
January 23	R$_x$	Aquarius
February 13	D	Aquarius
March 14	D	Pisces
April 1	D	Aries
April 15	D	Taurus
May 1	D	Gemini
May 21	R$_x$	Gemini
June 14	D	Gemini
July 9	D	Cancer
July 24	D	Leo
August 8	D	Virgo
August 28	D	Libra
September 19	R$_x$	Libra
October 11	D	Libra
November 3	D	Scorpio
November 21	D	Sagittarius
December 11	D	Capricorn

1983

DATE	MOTION	SIGN
January 1	D	Aquarius
January 7	R_x	Aquarius
January 12	R_x	Capricorn
January 27	D	Capricorn
February 14	D	Aquarius
March 7	D	Pisces
March 24	D	Aries
April 7	D	Taurus
May 1	R_x	Taurus
May 25	D	Taurus
June 14	D	Gemini
July 2	D	Cancer
July 16	D	Leo
August 1	D	Virgo
August 29	D	Libra
September 2	R_x	Libra
September 6	R_x	Virgo
September 25	D	Virgo
October 9	D	Libra
October 26	D	Scorpio
November 14	D	Sagittarius
December 4	D	Capricorn
December 22	R_x	Capricorn

1984

DATE	MOTION	SIGN
January 11	D	Capricorn
February 9	D	Aquarius
February 27	D	Pisces
March 14	D	Aries
April 1	D	Taurus
April 12	R$_x$	Taurus
April 25	R$_x$	Aries
May 5	D	Aries
May 15	D	Taurus
June 7	D	Gemini
June 22	D	Cancer
July 6	D	Leo
July 26	D	Virgo
August 15	R$_x$	Virgo
September 7	D	Virgo
October 1	D	Libra
October 18	D	Scorpio
November 6	D	Sagittarius
December 1	D	Capricorn
December 5	R$_x$	Capricorn
December 8	R$_x$	Sagittarius
December 24	D	Sagittarius

1985

DATE	MOTION	SIGN
January 11	D	Capricorn
February 1	D	Aquarius
February 19	D	Pisces
March 7	D	Aries
March 25	R$_x$	Aries
April 17	D	Aries
May 14	D	Taurus
May 31	D	Gemini
June 13	D	Cancer
June 30	D	Leo
July 28	R$_x$	Leo
August 21	D	Leo
September 7	D	Virgo
September 23	D	Libra
October 10	D	Scorpio
October 31	D	Sagittarius
November 18	R$_x$	Sagittarius
December 4	R$_x$	Scorpio
December 8	D	Scorpio
December 12	D	Sagittarius

1986

DATE	MOTION	SIGN
January 6	D	Capricorn
January 25	D	Aquarius
February 11	D	Pisces
March 3	D	Aries
March 7	R_x	Aries
March 11	R_x	Pisces
March 30	D	Pisces
April 17	D	Aries
May 7	D	Taurus
May 22	D	Gemini
June 5	D	Cancer
June 26	D	Leo
July 10	R_x	Leo
July 24	R_x	Cancer
August 3	D	Cancer
August 12	D	Leo
August 30	D	Virgo
September 15	D	Libra
October 4	D	Scorpio
November 2	R_x	Scorpio
November 22	D	Scorpio
December 10	D	Sagittarius
December 30	D	Capricorn

1987

DATE	MOTION	SIGN
January 17	D	Aquarius
February 4	D	Pisces
February 18	R$_x$	Pisces
March 12	D	Aquarius
March 14	D	Pisces
April 13	D	Aries
April 29	D	Taurus
May 13	D	Gemini
May 30	D	Cancer
June 21	R$_x$	Cancer
July 15	D	Cancer
August 7	D	Leo
August 22	D	Virgo
September 7	D	Libra
September 28	D	Scorpio
October 16	R$_x$	Scorpio
November 1	R$_x$	Libra
November 6	D	Libra
November 12	D	Scorpio
December 3	D	Sagittarius
December 22	D	Capricorn

1988

DATE	MOTION	SIGN
January 10	D	Aquarius
February 2	R$_x$	Aquarius
February 23	D	Aquarius
March 16	D	Pisces
April 5	D	Aries
April 20	D	Taurus
May 5	D	Gemini
June 1	R$_x$	Gemini
June 25	D	Gemini
July 12	D	Cancer
July 29	D	Leo
August 12	D	Virgo
August 31	D	Libra
September 29	R$_x$	Libra
October 20	D	Libra
November 6	D	Scorpio
November 25	D	Sagittarius
December 14	D	Capricorn

1989

DATE	MOTION	SIGN
January 3	D	Aquarius
January 16	R$_x$	Aquarius
January 29	R$_x$	Capricorn
February 6	D	Capricorn
February 14	D	Aquarius
March 10	D	Pisces
March 28	D	Aries
April 12	D	Taurus
April 30	D	Gemini
May 12	R$_x$	Gemini
May 29	R$_x$	Taurus
June 5	D	Taurus
June 12	D	Gemini
July 6	D	Cancer
July 20	D	Leo
August 5	D	Virgo
August 26	D	Libra
September 12	R$_x$	Libra
September 26	R$_x$	Virgo
October 4	D	Virgo
October 11	D	Libra
October 30	D	Scorpio
November 18	D	Sagittarius
December 7	D	Capricorn
December 31	R$_x$	Capricorn

DATE	MOTION	SIGN
January 20	D	Capricorn
February 12	D	Aquarius
March 3	D	Pisces
March 20	D	Aries
April 4	D	Taurus
April 23	R$_x$	Taurus
May 17	D	Taurus
June 12	D	Gemini
June 28	D	Cancer
July 12	D	Leo
July 29	D	Virgo
August 25	R$_x$	Virgo
September 17	D	Virgo
October 5	D	Libra
October 23	D	Scorpio
November 11	D	Sagittarius
December 2	D	Capricorn
December 15	R$_x$	Capricorn
December 26	R$_x$	Sagittarius

1991

DATE	MOTION	SIGN
January 3	D	Sagittarius
January 14	D	Capricorn
February 6	D	Aquarius
February 24	D	Pisces
March 12	D	Aries
April 4	R_x	Aries
April 28	D	Aries
May 17	D	Taurus
June 5	D	Gemini
June 19	D	Cancer
July 4	D	Leo
July 26	D	Virgo
August 8	R_x	Virgo
August 20	R_x	Leo
August 31	D	Leo
September 10	D	Virgo
September 28	D	Libra
October 15	D	Scorpio
November 4	D	Sagittarius
November 28	R_x	Sagittarius
December 18	D	Sagittarius

1992

DATE	MOTION	SIGN
January 10	D	Capricorn
January 30	D	Aquarius
February 16	D	Pisces
March 4	D	Aries
March 17	R$_x$	Aries
April 4	R$_x$	Pisces
April 9	D	Pisces
April 14	D	Aries
May 11	D	Taurus
May 27	D	Gemini
June 9	D	Cancer
June 27	D	Leo
July 20	R$_x$	Leo
August 13	D	Leo
September 3	D	Virgo
September 19	D	Libra
October 7	D	Scorpio
October 29	D	Sagittarius
November 11	R$_x$	Sagittarius
November 22	R$_x$	Scorpio
December 1	D	Scorpio
December 12	D	Sagittarius

1993

DATE	MOTION	SIGN
January 2	D	Capricorn
January 21	D	Aquarius
February 7	D	Pisces
February 28	R$_x$	Pisces
March 22	D	Pisces
April 15	D	Aries
May 4	D	Taurus
May 18	D	Gemini
June 2	D	Cancer
July 1	R$_x$	Cancer
July 26	D	Cancer
August 10	D	Leo
August 26	D	Virgo
September 11	D	Libra
October 1	D	Scorpio
October 26	R$_x$	Scorpio
November 15	D	Scorpio
December 7	D	Sagittarius
December 26	D	Capricorn

1994

DATE	MOTION	SIGN
January 14	D	Aquarius
February 1	D	Pisces
February 11	R_x	Pisces
February 21	Rx	Aquarius
March 5	D	Aquarius
March 18	D	Pisces
April 9	D	Aries
April 25	D	Taurus
May 10	D	Gemini
May 28	D	Cancer
June 12	R_x	Cancer
July 3	R_x	Gemini
July 7	D	Gemini
July 10	D	Cancer
August 3	D	Leo
August 18	D	Virgo
September 4	D	Libra
September 27	D	Scorpio
October 9	R_x	Scorpio
October 19	R_x	Libra
October 30	D	Libra
November 10	D	Scorpio
November 30	D	Sagittarius
December 19	D	Capricorn

1995

DATE	MOTION	SIGN
January 7	D	Aquarius
January 26	R$_x$	Aquarius
February 16	D	Aquarius
March 15	D	Pisces
April 2	D	Aries
April 17	D	Taurus
May 2	D	Gemini
May 24	R$_x$	Gemini
June 17	D	Gemini
July 10	D	Cancer
July 26	D	Leo
August 10	D	Virgo
August 29	D	Libra
September 22	R$_x$	Libra
October 14	D	Libra
November 4	D	Scorpio
November 23	D	Sagittarius
December 12	D	Capricorn

1996

DATE	MOTION	SIGN
January 1	D	Aquarius
January 10	R$_x$	Aquarius
January 17	R$_x$	Capricorn
January 30	D	Capricorn
February 15	D	Aquarius
March 7	D	Pisces
March 24	D	Aries
April 8	D	Taurus
May 4	R$_x$	Taurus
May 28	D	Taurus
June 14	D	Gemini
July 2	D	Cancer
July 16	D	Leo
August 1	D	Virgo
August 26	D	Libra
September 4	R$_x$	Libra
September 12	R$_x$	Virgo
September 26	D	Virgo
October 9	D	Libra
October 27	D	Scorpio
November 14	D	Sagittarius
December 4	D	Capricorn
December 24	R$_x$	Capricorn

1997

DATE	MOTION	SIGN
January 13	D	Capricorn
February 9	D	Aquarius
February 28	D	Pisces
March 16	D	Aries
April 1	D	Taurus
April 15	R_x	Taurus
May 5	R_x	Aries
May 8	D	Aries
May 12	D	Taurus
June 9	D	Gemini
June 24	D	Cancer
July 8	D	Leo
July 27	D	Virgo
August 18	R_x	Virgo
September 10	D	Virgo
October 2	D	Libra
October 19	D	Scorpio
November 7	D	Sagittarius
December 1	D	Capricorn
December 7	R_x	Capricorn
December 13	R_x	Sagittarius
December 27	D	Sagittarius

1998

DATE	MOTION	SIGN
January 12	D	Capricorn
February 2	D	Aquarius
February 20	D	Pisces
March 8	D	Aries
March 28	R$_x$	Aries
April 20	D	Aries
May 15	D	Taurus
June 1	D	Gemini
June 15	D	Cancer
July 1	D	Leo
July 31	R$_x$	Leo
August 24	D	Leo
September 8	D	Virgo
September 24	D	Libra
October 12	D	Scorpio
November 1	D	Sagittarius
November 21	R$_x$	Sagittarius
December 11	D	Sagittarius

1999

DATE	MOTION	SIGN
January 7	D	Capricorn
January 26	D	Aquarius
February 12	D	Pisces
March 3	D	Aries
March 10	R$_x$	Aries
March 18	R$_x$	Pisces
April 2	D	Pisces
April 18	D	Aries
May 9	D	Taurus
May 24	D	Gemini
June 7	D	Cancer
June 26	D	Leo
July 13	R$_x$	Leo
July 31	R$_x$	Cancer
August 6	D	Cancer
August 11	D	Leo
August 31	D	Virgo
September 16	D	Libra
October 5	D	Scorpio
October 31	D	Sagittarius
November 5	R$_x$	Sagittarius
November 10	R$_x$	Scorpio
November 25	D	Scorpio
December 11	D	Sagittarius
December 31	D	Capricorn

2000

DATE	MOTION	SIGN
January 19	D	Aquarius
February 5	D	Pisces
February 21	R$_x$	Pisces
March 15	D	Pisces
April 13	D	Aries
April 30	D	Taurus
May 14	D	Gemini
May 30	D	Cancer
June 23	R$_x$	Cancer
July 17	D	Cancer
August 7	D	Leo
August 22	D	Virgo
September 8	D	Libra
September 28	D	Scorpio
October 18	R$_x$	Scorpio
November 7	R$_x$	Libra
November 8	D	Scorpio
November 9	D	Scorpio
December 4	D	Sagittarius
December 23	D	Capricorn

2001

DATE	MOTION	SIGN
January 10	D	Aquarius
February 1	D	Pisces
February 4	R_x	Pisces
February 7	R_x	Aquarius
February 25	D	Aquarius
March 17	D	Pisces
April 6	D	Aries
April 22	D	Taurus
May 6	D	Gemini
June 4	R_x	Gemini
June 28	D	Gemini
July 13	D	Cancer
July 30	D	Leo
August 14	D	Virgo
September 1	D	Libra
October 2	R_x	Libra
October 23	D	Libra
November 8	D	Scorpio
November 26	D	Sagittarius
December 16	D	Capricorn

DATE	MOTION	SIGN
January 4	D	Aquarius
January 19	R_x	Aquarius
February 4	R_x	Capricorn
February 8	D	Capricorn
February 13	D	Aquarius
March 12	D	Pisces
March 29	D	Aries
April 13	D	Taurus
April 30	D	Gemini
May 15	R_x	Gemini
June 8	D	Gemini
July 7	D	Cancer
July 22	D	Leo
August 6	D	Virgo
August 27	D	Libra
September 15	R_x	Libra
October 2	R_x	Virgo
October 7	D	Virgo
October 11	D	Libra
November 1	D	Scorpio
November 19	D	Sagittarius
December 9	D	Capricorn

2003

DATE	MOTION	SIGN
January 2	R$_x$	Capricorn
January 23	D	Capricorn
February 13	D	Aquarius
March 5	D	Pisces
March 21	D	Aries
April 5	D	Taurus
April 26	R$_x$	Taurus
May 20	D	Taurus
June 13	D	Gemini
June 29	D	Cancer
July 13	D	Leo
July 30	D	Virgo
August 28	R$_x$	Virgo
September 20	D	Virgo
October 7	D	Libra
October 24	D	Scorpio
November 12	D	Sagittarius
December 3	D	Capricorn
December 17	R$_x$	Capricorn
December 31	R$_x$	Sagittarius

2004

DATE	MOTION	SIGN
January 6	D	Sagittarius
January 14	D	Capricorn
February 7	D	Aquarius
February 25	D	Pisces
March 12	D	Aries
April 1	D	Taurus
April 7	R_x	Taurus
April 13	R_x	Aries
April 30	D	Aries
May 16	D	Taurus
June 5	D	Gemini
June 20	D	Cancer
July 4	D	Leo
July 25	D	Virgo
August 10	R_x	Virgo
August 25	R_x	Leo
September 2	D	Leo
September 10	D	Virgo
September 28	D	Libra
October 16	D	Scorpio
November 4	D	Sagittarius
November 30	R_x	Sagittarius
December 20	D	Sagittarius

DATE	MOTION	SIGN
January 10	D	Capricorn
January 30	D	Aquarius
February 16	D	Pisces
March 5	D	Aries
March 20	R$_x$	Aries
April 12	D	Aries
May 12	D	Taurus
May 28	D	Gemini
June 11	D	Cancer
June 28	D	Leo
July 23	R$_x$	Leo
August 16	D	Leo
September 4	D	Virgo
September 20	D	Libra
October 8	D	Scorpio
October 30	D	Sagittarius
November 14	R$_x$	Sagittarius
November 26	R$_x$	Scorpio
December 4	D	Scorpio
December 13	D	Sagittarius

2006

DATE	MOTION	SIGN
January 4	D	Capricorn
January 23	D	Aquarius
February 9	D	Pisces
March 3	R$_x$	Pisces
March 25	D	Pisces
April 16	D	Aries
May 5	D	Taurus
May 20	D	Gemini
June 3	D	Cancer
June 29	D	Leo
July 5	R$_x$	Leo
July 11	R$_x$	Cancer
July 29	D	Cancer
August 11	D	Leo
August 28	D	Virgo
September 13	D	Libra
October 2	D	Scorpio
October 29	R$_x$	Scorpio
November 18	D	Scorpio
December 8	D	Sagittarius
December 28	D	Capricorn

2007

DATE	MOTION	SIGN
January 15	D	Aquarius
February 2	D	Pisces
February 14	R$_x$	Pisces
February 27	R$_x$	Aquarius
March 8	D	Aquarius
March 18	D	Pisces
April 11	D	Aries
April 27	D	Taurus
May 11	D	Gemini
May 29	D	Cancer
June 16	R$_x$	Cancer
July 10	D	Cancer
August 4	D	Leo
August 19	D	Virgo
September 5	D	Libra
September 27	D	Scorpio
October 12	R$_x$	Scorpio
October 24	R$_x$	Libra
November 2	D	Libra
November 11	D	Scorpio
December 1	D	Sagittarius
December 20	D	Capricorn

2008

DATE	MOTION	SIGN
January 8	D	Aquarius
January 29	R$_x$	Aquarius
February 19	D	Aquarius
March 15	D	Pisces
April 2	D	Aries
April 18	D	Taurus
May 3	D	Gemini
May 26	R$_x$	Gemini
June 19	D	Gemini
July 11	D	Cancer
July 26	D	Leo
August 10	D	Virgo
August 29	D	Libra
September 24	R$_x$	Libra
October 16	D	Libra
November 4	D	Scorpio
November 23	D	Sagittarius
December 12	D	Capricorn

2009

DATE	MOTION	SIGN
January 1	D	Aquarius
January 11	R_x	Aquarius
January 21	R_x	Capricorn
February 1	D	Capricorn
February 14	D	Aquarius
March 8	D	Pisces
March 26	D	Aries
April 9	D	Taurus
May 1	D	Gemini
May 7	R_x	Gemini
May 14	D	Taurus
May 31	D	Taurus
June 14	D	Gemini
July 4	D	Cancer
July 18	D	Leo
August 3	D	Virgo
August 26	D	Libra
September 7	R_x	Libra
September 18	R_x	Virgo
September 29	D	Virgo
October 10	D	Libra
October 28	D	Scorpio
November 16	D	Sagittarius
December 5	D	Capricorn
December 26	R_x	Capricorn

2010

DATE	MOTION	SIGN
January 15	D	Capricorn
February 10	D	Aquarius
March 1	D	Pisces
March 17	D	Aries
April 2	D	Taurus
April 18	R_x	Taurus
May 12	D	Taurus
June 10	D	Gemini
June 25	D	Cancer
July 9	D	Leo
July 28	D	Virgo
August 21	R_x	Virgo
September 13	D	Virgo
October 3	D	Libra
October 21	D	Scorpio
November 9	D	Sagittarius
December 1	D	Capricorn
December 10	R_x	Capricorn
December 18	R_x	Sagittarius
December 30	D	Sagittarius

2011

DATE	MOTION	SIGN
January 13	D	Capricorn
February 4	D	Aquarius
February 22	D	Pisces
March 9	D	Aries
March 31	R$_x$	Aries
April 23	D	Aries
May 16	D	Taurus
June 3	D	Gemini
June 17	D	Cancer
July 2	D	Leo
July 28	D	Virgo
August 3	R$_x$	Virgo
August 8	R$_x$	Leo
August 27	D	Leo
September 9	D	Virgo
September 26	D	Libra
October 13	D	Scorpio
November 2	D	Sagittarius
November 24	R$_x$	Sagittarius
December 14	D	Sagittarius

DATE	MOTION	SIGN
January 8	D	Capricorn
January 27	D	Aquarius
February 14	D	Pisces
March 2	D	Aries
March 12	R$_x$	Aries
March 23	R$_x$	Pisces
April 4	D	Pisces
April 17	D	Aries
May 9	D	Taurus
May 24	D	Gemini
June 7	D	Cancer
June 26	D	Leo
July 15	R$_x$	Leo
August 8	D	Leo
September 1	D	Virgo
September 17	D	Libra
October 5	D	Scorpio
October 29	D	Sagittarius
November 7	R$_x$	Sagittarius
November 14	R$_x$	Scorpio
November 27	D	Scorpio
December 11	D	Sagittarius
December 31	D	Capricorn

2013

DATE	MOTION	SIGN
January 19	D	Aquarius
February 5	D	Pisces
February 23	R$_x$	Pisces
March 18	D	Pisces
April 14	D	Aries
May 1	D	Taurus
May 16	D	Gemini
May 31	D	Cancer
June 26	R$_x$	Cancer
July 20	D	Cancer
August 8	D	Leo
August 24	D	Virgo
September 9	D	Libra
September 29	D	Scorpio
October 21	R$_x$	Scorpio
November 11	D	Scorpio
December 5	D	Sagittarius
December 24	D	Capricorn

2014

DATE	MOTION	SIGN
January 12	D	Aquarius
January 31	D	Pisces
February 7	R$_x$	Pisces
February 13	R$_x$	Aquarius
February 28	D	Aquarius
March 18	D	Pisces
April 7	D	Aries
April 23	D	Taurus
May 7	D	Gemini
May 29	D	Cancer
June 7	R$_x$	Cancer
June 17	R$_x$	Gemini
July 1	D	Gemini
July 13	D	Cancer
August 1	D	Leo
August 15	D	Virgo
September 2	D	Libra
September 28	D	Scorpio
October 4	R$_x$	Scorpio
October 10	R$_x$	Libra
October 26	D	Libra
November 9	D	Scorpio
November 28	D	Sagittarius
December 17	D	Capricorn

DATE	MOTION	SIGN
January 5	D	Aquarius
January 21	R$_x$	Aquarius
February 11	D	Aquarius
March 13	D	Pisces
March 31	D	Aries
April 15	D	Taurus
May 1	D	Gemini
May 19	R$_x$	Gemini
June 12	D	Gemini
July 8	D	Cancer
July 23	D	Leo
August 8	D	Virgo
August 27	D	Libra
September 17	R$_x$	Libra
October 9	D	Libra
November 2	D	Scorpio
November 21	D	Sagittarius
December 10	D	Capricorn

2016

DATE	MOTION	SIGN
January 2	D	Aquarius
January 5	R$_x$	Aquarius
January 9	R$_x$	Capricorn
January 26	D	Capricorn
February 14	D	Aquarius
March 5	D	Pisces
March 22	D	Aries
April 6	D	Taurus
April 28	R$_x$	Taurus
May 22	D	Taurus
June 13	D	Gemini
June 30	D	Cancer
July 14	D	Leo
July 30	D	Virgo
August 30	R$_x$	Virgo
September 22	D	Virgo
October 7	D	Libra
October 25	D	Scorpio
November 12	D	Sagittarius
December 3	D	Capricorn
December 19	R$_x$	Capricorn

2017

DATE	MOTION	SIGN
January 4	R$_x$	Sagittarius
January 8	D	Sagittarius
January 12	D	Capricorn
February 7	D	Aquarius
February 26	D	Pisces
March 14	D	Aries
March 31	D	Taurus
April 10	R$_x$	Taurus
April 20	R$_x$	Aries
May 3	D	Aries
May 16	D	Taurus
June 7	D	Gemini
June 21	D	Cancer
July 6	D	Leo
July 26	D	Virgo
August 13	R$_x$	Virgo
August 31	R$_x$	Leo
September 5	D	Leo
September 10	D	Virgo
September 30	D	Libra
October 17	D	Scorpio
November 6	D	Sagittarius
December 3	R$_x$	Sagittarius
December 23	D	Sagittarius

2018

DATE	MOTION	SIGN
January 11	D	Capricorn
January 31	D	Aquarius
February 18	D	Pisces
March 6	D	Aries
March 23	R$_x$	Aries
April 15	D	Aries
May 13	D	Taurus
May 30	D	Gemini
June 13	D	Cancer
June 29	D	Leo
July 26	R$_x$	Leo
August 19	D	Leo
September 6	D	Virgo
September 22	D	Libra
October 10	D	Scorpio
October 31	D	Sagittarius
November 17	R$_x$	Sagittarius
December 1	R$_x$	Scorpio
December 7	D	Scorpio
December 13	D	Sagittarius

2019

DATE	MOTION	SIGN
January 5	D	Capricorn
January 24	D	Aquarius
February 10	D	Pisces
March 5	R_x	Pisces
March 28	D	Pisces
April 17	D	Aries
May 6	D	Taurus
May 21	D	Gemini
June 5	D	Cancer
June 27	D	Leo
July 8	R_x	Leo
July 19	R_x	Cancer
August 1	D	Cancer
August 12	D	Leo
August 29	D	Virgo
September 14	D	Libra
October 3	D	Scorpio
October 31	R_x	Scorpio
November 21	D	Scorpio
December 9	D	Sagittarius
December 29	D	Capricorn

ACKNOWLEDGMENTS

FIRST, MY BELOVED LITERARY AGENT, CAROLE BIDNICK. When we first met at Rancho La Puerta in Mexico, I didn't have an astrology website or business card. She came to my presentation on astrology and immediately understood that I had a story to tell. She coached me, inspired me, and basically commanded me in the nicest Bidnick way to write a book proposal. I don't know many people who would have dedicated the time Carole gave me (two solid years), based simply on her steadfast belief that I was worth it. Thank you, dear Carole! You are first and foremost a gem of a human being, and I am very grateful.

Second, my brilliant editor at HarperElixir, Libby Edelson. From the start, I was impressed with her intellect and openness to approaching astrology from a new viewpoint.

As an editor, she dazzled me with her ability to make my writing the best it could possibly be. Over many months, she listened to stories about clients I had helped over the years. Through those tales, she understood that I wanted this book to be a place of solace: a book to turn to when a reader needed to make peace with why people think the way they do. Libby, you are a master with words, and I thank you for your kindness along the way. It has also been my good fortune to work with the entire team at Harper-Elixir, including Claudia Boutote, Suzanne Wickham, Ann Edwards, Anissa Elmerraji, and Noël Chrisman.

Finally, Victoria Larrea and all the guests at Rancho La Puerta who have come to my workshops. It took some bravery on Victoria's part to trust me with bringing astrology into the program. I understood her reluctance, and yet she trusted me when I told her I had a new way of explaining the theories behind astrology. Because of Victoria, thousands of ranch guests have had their lives changed through the power of this more compassionate use of astrology. Many thanks also to all those guests from Rancho La Puerta who have attended my workshops and spread the word. The ranch has always been a place of magic for me, and the people I have met there have been life savers and life changers. I am forever thankful.